The Elizabethan Theatre and

The Book of Sir Thomas More

The
Elizabethan
Theatre and
The Book of
Sir Thomas More

BY

SCOTT MCMILLIN

Cornell University Press

ITHACA AND LONDON

THIS BOOK HAS BEEN PUBLISHED WITH THE AID OF A GRANT FROM
THE HULL MEMORIAL PUBLICATION FUND OF CORNELL UNIVERSITY.

First published 1987 by Cornell University Press.

International Standard Book Number 0-8014-2008-3
Library of Congress Catalog Card Number 86-47996

Printed in the United States of America

*Librarians: Library of Congress cataloging information
appears on the last page of the book.*

Contents

PREFACE

7

1. *Locations*

15

2. *Parts for Actors: Casting the Play*

34

3. *The Original Play: Acting Company and Date*

53

4. *The Revised Play: Acting Company and Date*

74

5. *Staging the Play*

96

6. *Staging at the Rose*

113

7. *Hand D*

135

CONTENTS

APPENDIX

Minimum Casting Charts

161

INDEX

165

Preface

The manuscript Elizabethan play called *Sir Thomas More* has intrigued scholars for over a century because three of its pages may have been written by Shakespeare. My purpose is to set the manuscript in a new framework by beginning not with questions about authorship but with questions about the Elizabethan theatre: what kind of theatrical manuscript is this? how would it have been used in the theatre? how large a company does it require? which parts can be doubled? what kind of staging does it imply? why did the play have to be revised? This is not the first time these questions have been raised, but it appears to be the first time they have been separated from the possibility of Shakespearean authorship long enough to receive answers for themselves. Those answers I then turn into a new context for addressing major issues of identification—not the identification of authors, in the first instance, but the identification of the acting companies for which the manuscript was originally written and subsequently revised. *Those* identifications, it may finally be admitted, do bear on questions of authorship, even on the

7

question of Shakespearean authorship, but I have done my best to postpone such considerations to the final chapter, and to hedge them with speculations inimical to Bardolatry.

When I first studied the *More* manuscript, it seemed coherent and purposeful, and I was surprised to learn that exactly the opposite opinion held sway in the volumes of scholarship devoted to the authorship question. Experts were deeming unfinished and incoherent a manuscript that seemed to me completely ready to serve a particular function in the theatre. Since I was obviously not a brighter reader than the others, I thought it must be the difference in perspective that caused the difference in reading. Chapters 1 and 2 work out the terms of this observation and attempt to demonstrate that the manuscript was composed and revised to serve particular purposes in the theatre. I hope the results will appeal to textual scholars as well as to theatre historians, for if I am right about the *More* manuscript, we are confronted with a type of promptbook which has been occasionally theorized but never described. This is a promptbook prepared for the copying of the actors' parts. Every Elizabethan play-text must have passed through this stage, yet textual scholars, lacking examples of such intermediate promptbooks, have paid little heed to this part of the process. If I am right about the *More* manuscript, it will deserve fresh thinking on the part of textual scholars.

One puzzle continued to bother me while I was working from the theatrical point of view. It was clear that the so-called Additions to the manuscript were intended to solve the problem of casting a large play within the capabilities of a normal Elizabethan acting company, but I found it odd that the writers of the original version were content to establish this problem in the first place, without taking steps to solve it themselves. One of the original writers was Anthony Munday—identity questions cannot be ruled out altogether—and Anthony Munday knew well enough not to produce an outlandishly oversized play that would have to be revised before the casting could be done. There are nearly sixty speaking parts in the original *Sir Thomas*

More, with crowd scenes to boot: costumes alone would be a major expense. Rather than assume that Munday and the others were incompetent, I set out to see if they could have been writing for an unusually large company (which was perhaps not available to the revisers), and I discovered that we are nearly speechless when it comes to determining the size of the various acting companies. We know who were the principal actors and sharers in some companies, but we can estimate the overall size of a troupe only by taking up the texts it performed, counting the roles, counting the lines spoken in each role, spacing out the doubling possibilities (for the companies depended on heavy doubling for economy), and counting everything again to make sure. Is it surprising that this tallying has not been done for the plays of Anthony Munday? Only for Shakespeare has much character and line counting been done, and what I needed was a systematic gathering of evidence across the range of Elizabethan drama, which was written mainly by Anthony Munday and his fellows.

So I counted for myself and asked others to check my work by counting too. We took up all Elizabethan public-theatre plays written between 1580 and 1610, and counted. I shall spare the reader a description of this work. The results are in Chapter 3, where they amount to new evidence, I think, about the acting company for which the original *Sir Thomas More* was intended. Chapter 4 discusses the company for which the revision seems to have been undertaken, as much as a decade later. The general point I wish to stress from this experience is that until we know the theatrical characteristics of each acting company, we do not know some of the basic facts of Elizabethan theatre history. We find it convenient to blend all the professional companies together in order to generalize about "the" Elizabethan theatre, but lost in that process is the possibility—I think it virtually a certainty—that each company had its own political and theatrical characteristics. I have glanced at the political characteristics of the relevant companies in Chapter 3, but the main purposes of Chapters 3 and 4 are to describe the casting size of

Sir Thomas More for the first time, to develop a preliminary context of casting information about the relevant companies so that the *More* manuscript can be nudged toward its historical place in the business of the playhouses, and to call attention to the large project for which all my counting is but an improvised introduction. A complete account of each company's repertory, to determine casting and doubling patterns, seems to me the most obvious need in Elizabethan theatre history today.

Staging is another theatrical characteristic by which the companies should be differentiated. Theatre historians have accomplished much in the study of individual theatres, but the possibility that companies had different styles of staging has not been explored except for the Chamberlain's/King's men, formed in 1594. I have opened this subject in Chapters 5 and 6, the one being an examination of the staging intentions in *Sir Thomas More*, the other of staging intentions in the repertory and the theatre where I think *More* was originally intended to be performed. Again, I intend this specific analysis to open the larger issue for theatre history. We are accustomed to studying individual theatres in terms of staging, but no one seems to consider that individual acting companies may have had their own styles of staging. The evidence lies before us—it has been there for four hundred years, and it is the plays themselves.

If the early chapters that follow are addressed to textual scholars, in other words, my aim is really to reach my colleagues in theatre history and to say that we have much work of our own to do. Ultimately, I hope the division between textual scholar and theatre historian can be softened so that the two disciplines can be brought into a much-needed cooperation. The topics were separated in the late nineteenth and early twentieth centuries as a way of establishing a scientific basis for each pursuit, but each pursuit is now difficult to follow from the specialized perspective of the other. In this regard, I wish to acknowledge the productive research seminars in theatre history and textual studies held each year at the convention of the Shakespeare Association of America. These are, alas, separate seminars, but the number of us who cross from one to the other as participants and auditors suggests to me that a merger of our interests is already under way.

If in the pages that follow I seem to be teasing my textually devoted colleagues for not having been stagestruck enough to see one Elizabethan manuscript for what it is, they will understand that I am only trying to provoke interest in developing a collaboration of our disciplines. I know that textual scholars are avid for the playhouse, just as those who happen to know me know that I spend more time in libraries than in theatres. Both are good places for all of us. The library where the basic work for this book was done is the Manuscript Students' Room of the British Library. That my opening chapter defines this as the wrong location for thinking about *Sir Thomas More* does not reduce my obligation to the very helpful Supervisors and staff of that archive, who answered my needs at every turn and even created a few that I was unaware of.

Many friends and colleagues have supported the work of this book. T. H. Howard-Hill and Eugene Waith provided occasions for me to present my research as it progressed. Herbert Berry, S. P. Cerasano, Terry Corsberg, Richard Hosley, T. H. Howard-Hill, William Ingram, T. J. King, Roslyn Knutson, G. R. Proudfoot, Gary Taylor, and David Thurn responded to my questions and pleas for help with generous expertise. David Bevington and George Walton Williams gave useful commentary in reading the manuscript for Cornell University Press. The editorial expertise of Kay Scheuer has been a great benefit. I am grateful to the National Endowment for the Humanities and the Cornell Humanities Research Fund for financial support. For permission to reprint material from an earlier article, *"The Book of Sir Thomas More:* A Theatrical View," © 1970 by the University of Chicago, I thank the editors of *Modern Philology* and the University of Chicago Press, its publisher.

SCOTT MCMILLIN

Ithaca, New York

The Elizabethan Theatre and
The Book of Sir Thomas More

1

Locations

Now that three generations of reasonable and crafty scholars have been able to study the *Book of Sir Thomas More* in Greg's edition of 1911,[1] the central question remaining to be answered is: what use was this manuscript intended to serve? This strikes me as a basic historical question, the question of use, and if I am right to assert that it has not been answered, we should not only undertake the task immediately, but also speculate on the disinclination of others to do so.

The location of the manuscript may be the heart of the problem. For over two centuries *The Book of Sir Thomas More* has reposed in what is now called the British Library, where it is classed as MS. Harley 7368 and is preserved, page by page, in transparent plastic jackets so sturdy that one could use them to lay out a model of an Elizabethan stage. The manuscript was intended for a drastically different location. It was intended for

1. W. W. Greg, ed., *The Book of Sir Thomas More* (Oxford: Malone Society, 1911). Hereafter all references to the play pertain to this edition unless otherwise noted.

an Elizabethan stage, in fact, although considering the way original manuscripts were actually employed in the theatre, we should say it was intended for a backstage area, the tiring-house as the Elizabethans called it, where it would have been worked over and readied to the point of serving some purpose in the rehearsing or performing of the play. I think it has been brought to the point where the parts for actors could have been copied from it, but that is to anticipate the argument a little.

The Manuscript Students' Room of the British Library holds two advantages over an Elizabethan playhouse: it exists, and it preserves manuscripts very carefully. So obvious are these benefits that they might lull scholars into forgetting that advantages are always nagged by corresponding disadvantages, the disadvantages in this case being that as a real place the Manuscript Students' Room tends to put imagined places like an Elizabethan playhouse out of mind, and as a careful preserver of manuscripts it tends to define manuscripts as things to be kept, not things to be used. Try using the manuscript in the Manuscript Students' Room as (let us say) Edward Alleyn would have used the copies made from it in a theatre—declaim its text, that is, so as to draw the wonder of pleasure-seeking Londoners from all walks of life—and the Supervisors of the Manuscript Students' Room will make the problem apparent at once.

In the British Library, writing is held for posterity. In an Elizabethan playhouse, speech was used for the moment. In its present location, *The Book of Sir Thomas More* has been seen as an "authored" document, a form of communication between writers and readers, and it has been studied by readers whose paramount concern is to learn the identities of the writers. As R. W. Chambers once remarked, the problem is to get more interesting names for Hands A, B, C, D, E, and S.[2] This line of investigation has indeed produced interesting names—Anthony Munday, Henry Chettle, Thomas Heywood?, Thomas Dekker, Wil-

2. R. W. Chambers, *Man's Unconquerable Mind* (London: Cape, 1939), p. 213.

liam Shakespeare?—but it has resulted in the assumption that the manuscript is a collection of paleographical clues rather than a coherent theatrical document. The theatre is irrelevant to paleographical investigation. The theatre presents ephemera, and it employs authored documents only as necessary devices in rehearsal and backstage management. The prompt copy of a successful Elizabethan play would have been kept handy against the occasion of a revival, of course, but the resemblance of such storage to the preservation afforded in the British Library may be judged by noting that virtually all promptbooks, of the thousands that must have been kept by the actors, have disappeared.

May it be said that a concern for authorship in the Manuscript Students' Room is also a concern for authority? I am punning a bit, but not for the sake of frivolity. Theatrical performance in some cultures runs counter to authority, a point that would have been recognized by London magistrates of the 1590s, and when a scholar holds a page of *The Book of Sir Thomas More* up to the light in the Manuscript Students' Room (the plastic jacket notwithstanding), the alarm of the Supervisors is a sign that authority is their first concern. Prior to Greg's edition, readers of the manuscript hardly ever thought about theatricality, and in concentrating on the identities of the authors instead, they found themselves concentrating on the one true authority figure involved in all the handwriting, the Master of the Revels, Edmund Tilney. Tilney dealt the original play a harsh blow by writing in the margin of the first page of dialogue that about a third of the play—the uprising of Ill May-Day—had to be cut out and reported in narration.

Scholars before Greg supposed that it must have been an effort to satisfy the authority of Tilney that caused five writers to patch and pad the original text with revisions. Greg made it clear, however, that the revisions bear very little relation to the censorship, and his opinion—that "the bulk of the additional matter . . . can have nothing whatever to do with the censor, being obviously due solely to dramatic considerations"—has been generally accepted by later scholars.[3] This could have been a useful decentering of the authorship question. Yet "dramatic considerations" is one of those phrases which can gain a niche in scholarship without taking on any precise meaning, and that seems to have occurred in regard to *The Book of Sir Thomas More.* Although it is obvious that one of the writers, the one known to us as Hand D, was intent upon increasing the eloquence by which More was supposed to have quelled the Ill May-Day riots, we have no exact knowledge about the purposes behind 560 additional lines which four other writers supplied to the original text.

Moreover, the urgent concern for authorship and identity has led the expert readers into a serious mistake. There is a widespread and unexamined notion that because this theatrical manuscript does not *look* as though it was meant to be preserved, it must have been compiled in a slapdash manner only to be left incomplete. In his edition Greg could discern "no attempt . . . to sew the loose ends into decent continuity" (p. xv), and in reviewing the matter fifty years later Harold Jenkins insisted that the play was "reduced to incoherence" and left "unfinished and chaotic." For Dover Wilson, "as it stands, the play could not have been acted," and for T. W. Baldwin, "after all hands and the cook (except the original author) had done their endeavors, the surviving mess was the result."[4]

Such impressions are wrong, and my goal is both to show that the manuscript has been designed for the production of a coherent and actable play and to argue that the date of that play,

3. Greg edition, p. xv.
4. Harold Jenkins, "Supplement to Greg's Edition of *Sir Thomas More,*" in Malone Society *Collections,* vol. 6 (Oxford: Malone Society, 1961), p. 185; J. Dover Wilson, "The New Way with Shakespeare's Texts III," *Shakespeare Survey,* 9 (1956), 72; T. W. Baldwin, *On the Literary Genetics of Shakespeare's Plays: 1592–1594* (Urbana: Univ. of Illinois Press, 1959), p. 270n. W. J. Lawrence should be mentioned as one who argued for the theatrical coherence of the manuscript, but his interpretation that it served as a promptbook was disapproved by Greg (see *Times Literary Supplement,* July 1, 1920, p. 421, followed by July 8, p. 440, July 15, p. 456, July 29, p. 488, and September 2, p. 568).

along with the circumstances of its revision, can be determined by imagining a different location for the manuscript—not the British Library, with its inherent bias for authorship and posterity, but the Elizabethan theatre, where writing was turned to speech and gesture in the interests of play. *The Book of Sir Thomas More* can be seen for what it is by setting aside questions of authorship and pursuing questions of the theatre instead. Authorship will mislead. Those who place authors first expect books to be tidy and well-made. They will have trouble with the disarray of *The Book of Sir Thomas More* (one of the pages is even misplaced), and they will feel that the manuscript is incoherent. Those who look to the theatre first are in position to know better—to know, for example, that behind the most coherent stage performance lies debris of all sorts, including textual debris. Walk backstage after a good performance and you will see the debris at once, and if you want to see textual debris, ask for the original prompt copy, the one that was used at the beginning of rehearsals. Should the play in question be an original work, the earliest prompt copy will look a bit like *The Book of Sir Thomas More*. Should the play in question be a work written ten years ago, and now revised for a different acting company, its rehearsal book will look a lot like *The Book of Sir Thomas More*, although the paper will not be as interesting.

The first task is to study the plainest of matters, for it is with these that the mistakes have been made. We will begin with the arrangement of the manuscript leaves, the placing of the insertions, the clarity of the implied dramatic action, the extent of such errors as remain. This is hard, detailed work, but along with the desire to set the record straight goes the hope that a pattern will emerge from the details. Under patient examination, the remaining errors in *The Book of Sir Thomas More* will be found to belong to one type. The result is that they can be thought about instead of brushed aside in a broad complaint about the incoherence of the manuscript, and when they are thought about I believe they tell us what position *The Book of Sir Thomas More* held in the business of the playhouse. Textual scholars should find this phase of our work purposeful, for it appears that the manuscript is something more than a collection of "foul papers," as first drafts were sometimes called, but is a sort of preliminary promptbook, brought to a particular stage of completion in the process of rehearsal. Every Elizabethan play must have passed through this stage of completion, although textual scholarship has rather ignored it.

The play divides into three units, and it will be well to examine the condition of each part in turn. The first section presents the Ill May-Day uprising of 1517, which dramatically (and unhistorically) becomes the occasion for More's rise to power. In the manuscript, the original version of the first three scenes, although heavily censored by Tilney, bears no sign of theatrical revision. On folio 5b, however, all of scene iv and the beginning of scene v have been marked for omission, and the following one or more leaves have been torn out. A large cross in the margin of folio 5b shows that the rejected scenes were to be replaced by Addition II, which is marked by a similar cross on its first page and which runs continuously from folio 7a through folio 9a. The pages of revision would be exactly in place were it not for the intrusion of Addition I, which has been misplaced as folio 6: this is the only mistake in the ordering of pages as the manuscript now stands. Between folio 9a (the end of Addition II) and folio 10a (the resumption of the original text) the joining has been perfected. From this point through the end of the insurrection (fol. 11b), the original leaves remain intact.

Despite the lacuna after folio 5b, we can be fairly certain of the original arrangement of action. Scene iv shows one phase of the May-Day uprising—John Lincoln's rousing of English craftsmen against the foreigners in St. Martin's. Scene v, which breaks off after nineteen lines, was to represent another phase of the rising, in which a group of apprentices wounded Sir John Munday when he attempted to curtail their May-Day games. The lacuna occurs before Munday's entrance, but his skirmish with the apprentices is described by Hall, whom the play follows closely in this section, and the incident is recounted in the canceled lines 68–75 of Addition II. What originally followed the apprentice scene we cannot be sure; but there is no reason to suppose that the order of scenes differed from the order of the revised version, in which More meets several authorities to recommend a parley with the rioters and then proceeds to conduct the parley brilliantly himself.[5]

With this outline in mind, we may observe several points about the three scenes of revision which appear consecutively in Addition II. In the first, Hand B has copied the original scene iv, adding nine brief speeches for a "Clown," who is to take the place of a mute character in the original version. Scene v (the apprentice scene) disappears entirely in revision, so that the action moves directly to the meeting of More and the higher authorities, which is in Hand C. A false start brings Sir John Munday into this scene to report his skirmish with the apprentices, but these lines have been marked for omission, and the action proceeds with no further reference to Munday. Then follows the long and well-known scene by Hand D, in which More quells the insurgents with his speeches of substantial conservatism. As the insurgents yield to More's persuasions, D's portion of the revision ends, and the original manuscript carries through scenes vi and vii to the end of the rebellion section. Hand B, ever busy with his Clown, has added five pieces of comic dialogue in the margins of these original pages.

The action of the first section of the play is essentially finished and ready to be rehearsed and played. The speech prefixes are also in good condition. Hand C has had to make about a dozen corrections and additions to Hand D's contribution in Addition II, but he has done the job thoroughly. The bit of dialogue which Hand B wrote in the margin of folio 11a lacks some pre-

---

5. The sources are well studied in Vittorio Gabrieli and Giorgio Melchiori, eds., *The Book of Sir Thomas More* (Bari: Adriatica, 1981). To be precise, the uprising is based on Hall as recorded in Holinshed. In *"The Booke of Sir Thomas Moore* Re-examined," *Studies in Philology*, 69 (1972), 167–191, Peter Blayney speculates that the original version may have included other episodes, in which the character Crofts would have appeared along with the authorities to whom he reported. See also the article by Melchiori in note 6 below.

fixes for the Clown and the Sheriff, but it is clear who is speaking in all cases, and a prompter or a theatre scribe working on the manuscript would be in no danger of mistaking the speakers.[6]

There is no doubt that this section of the play, in its revised form, is complete and coherent. As A. W. Pollard remarked, these scenes would by themselves form an effective short play about the May-Day rising.[7] A few small errors, however, remain uncorrected, and exactly what these are is instructive. The dialogue has been brought into good theatrical condition, and aside from lines that violate precise iambic pentameter (hardly any texts are perfect in this regard), I can find little that should have been altered. One of Hand D's phrases (Addition II, l. 131) has not been reconciled with a deletion in the same line, and Surrey's speech beginning at line 324 in the original text suffers from tangled writing, although the sense is discernible. The deletion at lines 726–730 should include line 725. These are minor matters, the sort of flaw which occurs regularly in Elizabethan play texts and which actors are able to smooth over in performance.

One final example will make the point. Hand C misunderstood D's lines at Addition II, lines 235–237. D's original lines make good sense if one understands (as Harold Jenkins and G. Blakemore Evans did in their modernized texts) that a stop must be inserted after the word "feet" in the fourth line quoted. Here is the modernized verson:

> Wash your foul minds with tears, and those same hands
> That you like rebels lift against the peace
> Lift up for peace, and your unreverent knees,
> Make them your feet. To kneel to be forgiven

---

6. Giorgio Melchiori criticizes some of C's prefixes, but this is a matter of taste. See "Hand D in *Sir Thomas More*: An Essay in Misinterpretation," *Shakespeare Survey*, 38 (1985), 107–109.

7. Alfred W. Pollard, ed., *Shakespeare's Hand in the Play of Sir Thomas More* (Cambridge: Cambridge Univ. Press, 1923), p. 3.

> Is safer wars than ever you can make,
> Whose discipline is riot.

Clear enough: Inelegant, but clear. But without the stop after "feet," which is how D left the line, there occurs the gibberish that C corrected by placing a stop after "forgiven," crossing out the next several lines, and inserting "Tell me but this" to bridge the gap that he had created:

> Wash your foul minds with tears, and those same hands
> That you like rebels lift against the peace,
> Lift up for peace, and your unreverent knees,
> Make them your feet to kneel to be forgiven.
> Tell me but this, what rebel captain. . . .

In either case, the meaning is clear, but this heavily scored part of the manuscript surely contributed to the mistaken impression of "wild disarray," and it should be salutary to realize that the only actual mistake made in the writing was D's omission of one stop.[8]

In only one respect are the writers prone to mistakes: the stage directions are often wrong. In his share of Addition II, Hand B included no directions at all. The omissions are especially odd in that B was repeating the dialogue from the original text of scene iv, while adding the new lines for the Clown, and yet he did not repeat the entrance and exist directions that stood in the original text. For example, when George Betts says in the original (ll. 434–435) "Let some of us enter the straungers houses, / and if we finde them there, then bringe them foorth," the obvious exit direction follows: "ex. some and Sher"; but

---

8. My quotations follow *The Riverside Shakespeare*, ed. G. Blakemore Evans et al. (Boston: Houghton Mifflin, 1974), which benefited from Harold Jenkins's modernization in *William Shakespeare: The Complete Works*, ed. C. J. Sisson (New York: Harper, 1953). "Wild disarray" is from Carol A. Chillington, "Playwrights at Work: Henslowe's, Not Shakespeare's, *Book of Sir Thomas More*," *English Literary Renaissance*, 10 (1980), 439–479. See also Melchiori, "Hand D in *Sir Thomas More*," pp. 104–106.

when B copies those two lines, he omits the exit direction. B may have been writing from dictation, for he often changes the original spelling, and perhaps only the dialogue was being read to him; but the point remains that the original stage directions did not matter in the process of B's work.

Hand D did undertake one stage direction in his contribution to Addition II, and Peter Blayney, noting that it is "probably the clearest and most prominent interim direction in the whole MS," has suggested that the writer was more concerned than his collaborators with making things clear for the actors.[9] At the same time it must be admitted that Hand D either fouled the direction by omitting Sir Thomas More from it or else knew of an earlier entrance direction that has disappeared. D was certainly intent on More's rhetoric, but nowhere does he bring the hero onto the stage. Blayney's shrewd comment about D's concern for theatrical clarity leaves us wondering why that concern did not extend to accurate entrance directions.

Moreover, Hand C—who as the coordinator of revision would be expected to set the directions right—leaves errors in the stage directions too. On folio 5a, where the original text is interrupted for Addition II, he wrote a marginal entrance direction—"Enter Lincolne Betts Williamson Doll" (ll. 410–412)—as an introduction for Hand B's revision, but he omitted two necessary characters (Sherwin and one of the brothers Betts— although perhaps his "Betts" is meant to be plural). Further, he did not supply the entrance and exit direction which B omitted in the first revised scene; and in introducing the subsequent episode, after eliminating all traces of Sir John Munday from the dialogue, he left Munday's name in the opening direction. In Hand D's section of Addition II, he supplied a redundant entrance for the Sergeant at Arms (l. 139) and did not complete the one direction D attempted.

9. Blayney, *"The Booke of Sir Thomas Moore* Re-examined," p. 178. D's knowledge of an earlier entrance direction has recently been proposed by G. Melchiori, "Hand D in Sir Thomas More," pp. 109–110.

In other words, there is a pattern to the evidence. The speech prefixes and dialogue of this opening section of the revised *Sir Thomas More* are as accurate as Elizabethan plays normally are, but the stage directions are distinctly unfinished. Why should a play manuscript be finished in all respects except stage directions?—that is the question beginning to take shape.

In the middle section of the play the original scheme of action is difficult to infer, owing to a lacuna of one or more leaves after folio 11. Peter Blayney has convincingly argued that the Erasmus scene and the long-haired ruffian scene, which are merged in the revision, originally stood apart from one another and may have been separated by a scene of narrative linkage.[10] The separate Erasmus and ruffian scenes would then have been followed by the third in this series of humorous episodes, More's extemporaneous performance in a play intended to grace a visit by the Lord Mayor. All of the original material has been canceled except for the Mayor's scene. As the revised manuscript stands, the middle section begins with the continuous series of Additions III, IV, and V, which have the effect of combining the Erasmus and ruffian episodes (Additions III and IV) and narrating both the departure of Erasmus and the approach of the Lord Mayor (Addition V). This is the part of the play in which the most straightforward material has been misread by generations of scholars. We shall take up the episodes in order, as they stand in the revised text.

Addition III is More's twenty-one-line soliloquy ("It is in heaven that I am thus and thus"), which C copied on a separate sheet and pasted accurately to the bottom half of folio 11b. As Greg noted in his edition (p. 79n.), the soliloquy was intended to lead into Addition IV. Unfortunately, Greg went on to say that the speech "has no connection with what follows," an opinion echoed by R. C. Bald's later statement that the soliloquy was written "in response to a request for an effective speech for More that could be inserted at any appropriate point." A further variation

---

10. Blayney, "*The Booke of Sir Thomas Moore* Re-examined," pp. 170–171.

comes from Blayney, who thinks that the speech is so good that it was kept with the intention of sticking it somewhere, perhaps in the midst of the preceding scene.[11]

Such ideas are wrong. The soliloquy belongs exactly where it stands in the manuscript and makes a definite connection with what follows. The speech is More's meditation on the dangers and false allurements of high rank. Wearing the robes of the chancellorship, beholding the purse and mace symbolic of his position, he observes that one must fear the trappings of honor, office, wealth, and calling. A moment later, at the beginning of Addition IV, he will assign his robes and symbols of office to one of his servants, in order that a mock Chancellor may welcome Erasmus. Acted by itself, as the original version intended it to be, the false welcoming of Erasmus is pleasant nonsense. Joined to More's meditation on the false appearances of office, it becomes a moment of pointed irony. When the servant says "I have practised yo[r] Lordshipps shift so well that I thinke I shall grow prowd my Lord," we are aware that More has just rehearsed to himself the dangers attending on pride of office. More's reply to the servant—"tis fitt thou shouldst wax prowd or ells thoult nere / be neere allied to greatnes"—takes on a rueful tone, partly because he has just disavowed pride for himself and partly because a different quality, a personal and skeptical quality that might be another form of pride, will render tragic his own alliance to greatness. "Ile see If greate Erasmus can distinguishe / meritt and outward Cerimony," is More's explanation for the disguise trick. His soliloquy has just shown his concern for this distinction, which will eventually prove the leading quality of his public career. In the context of the soliloquy, in other words, the welcoming of Erasmus changes from a pointless piece of amusement to a short enactment of More's serious concern for his public role. The coordination of Additions III and IV contains more than a connection between two pieces of revision;

11. R. C. Bald, "Addition III of *Sir Thomas More*," *Review of English Studies*, 7 (1931), 67. Blayney, *"The Booke of Sir Thomas Moore* Re-examined," pp. 179–180.

it also provides the most thoughtful moment in a play which sometimes verges on historical simplemindedness.[12]

Addition IV, running to 242 lines, is the longest revision in this section of the play. It combines two scenes that seem to have been discrete in the original, with the result that More's encounter with Erasmus is punctuated by his episode with the shaggy ruffian Faulkner. The action is quite clear, and only one point requires our attention now. The bulk of the addition was copied by C on folios 12a through the first half of 13b. A thirty-line conclusion to the scene was added by Hand E on the bottom half of folio 13b. While Hand E's part of the addition has always been recognized as an afterthought, the exact evidence needs to be described. Several of C's attempts at an exit direction on folio 13b indicate that the scene was progressively lengthened. In the margin at lines 203–204, C first wrote "Enter a messenger heere," showing that he was already looking ahead to Addition V, which begins with a messenger. That marginal direction has been crossed out, however, and Addition IV continues with seven more lines of dialogue in Hand C. Then at line 211, C wrote "exit," presumably to end the scene there, but again the direction has been crossed out. At this point E's thirty-line conclusion fills out the page, and the scene finally ends. It would seem, then, that Hands C and E discovered reasons to lengthen the scene's conclusion as they worked. The purposes behind this bit of patching concern the casting and staging of the play, but the point cannot be properly explained until later.

Addition V, which follows immediately, is a tiny device that has been strangely misread. Because of the combination of the Faulkner and Erasmus episodes, the revisers were obviously forced to write a few lines of linkage which would introduce the next major scene—the Lord Mayor's visit to More—with a mini-

12. For further discussion see Charles R. Forker and Joseph Candido, "Wit, Wisdom, and Theatricality in the *Book of Sir Thomas More,*" *Shakespeare Studies,* 13 (1980), 85–104. For a more general defense of the soliloquy's position, see J. M. Nosworthy, "Shakespeare and *Sir Thomas More,*" *Review of English Studies,* n.s. 6 (1955), 12–25.

mum of confusion. And so, working partly from a draft by Hand B, Hand C copied and fitted into place some twenty-five lines between More and a messenger. The lines are strangely distributed on folio 14a, with the messenger's speech in the margin and More's reply on a pasted sheet, but the order of the dialogue is quite clear. The messenger announces that the Lord Mayor has unexpectedly arrived for a banquet. More responds gladly, explaining that he needs an occasion of good cheer now that Erasmus has departed. For some reason, Greg complained that "such a crude insertion is manifestly impossible, for the action is not continuous" (p. xii). Since the only point of Addition V is to make the action literally continuous, this is a strange remark. In another note Greg asserted that the messenger scene "leaves no time for the dinner" (p. 89n); this is plainly wrong, for the dinner has not yet begun. Since Greg's complaints have been picked up by such other reliable scholars as Harold Jenkins and R. C. Bald, one must insist upon the obvious.[13] Addition V is certainly an awkward device of explanation, but it *does* explain: Erasmus has departed; time has passed; the Lord Mayor has suddenly arrived for a banquet which will have to be improvised; and More's whimsical sense of decorum awakens in this strange impromptu situation.

Once these points are understood, the original play scene (fols. 14b–17a) fits easily into the context of the revisions. The traveling players are especially welcome to More because their play will help to fill an awkward interval while the banquet is being hurried together. The interlude itself is one of those pieces of slight cleverness which seem to have been the highest reach of Hand S's art. When More takes on the role of Good

13. See Jenkins's text, note to act 3, scene 2, in Sisson's edition of Shakespeare, p. 1253, along with Bald, "*The Booke of Sir Thomas More* and Its Problems," *Shakespeare Survey*, 2 (1949), 49. The confusion may arise from ll. 893–900 of the original, which at a glance might suggest that the banquet has already been served; but the meaning is that the Mayor's entourage, finding no preparations under way at the banquet table, have resorted to the fireside.

Counsel in a play that is to show the marriage of Wit to Wisdom he is enacting the central concern of his own public life, and his improvised line of advice, "judge not things by the outwarde showe" (l. 1131), relates to his motive in the earlier welcoming of Erasmus. There is no serious probing of these matters, but the scene is written with superficial alertness to its bearing on the entire action. At the end of the original scene (fol. 17a) a marginal note and symbol relate to Addition VI, written by Hand B and inserted as folio 16. This is an extension of the players' scene, in which the performer of Wit proves his name by revealing the petty thievery of a servant. The addition also shows More's departure for an emergency meeting of the council, thus closing this section of the play with a hint of the downfall to come.

If it is clear that this heavily revised section contains no "manifestly impossible" insertions and provides a coherent arrangement of action, we may notice that the several errors remaining in the manuscript are similar to those in the first section. Again the dialogue and prefixes are clear, but the stage directions have not been fully corrected. The dialogue, read carefully, requires no important changes, although the marginal "*et tu Erasmus an Diabolus*" (Addition IV, l. 150) has not been incorporated. In Addition V, sections of dialogue have been joined by repeated lines (l. 8 and l. 26), but this intentional device causes no confusion. The duplication of "more" at Addition VI, line 56, may be an error, although it could form part of a pun. If Addition VI, line 5 means that the banquet has already ended, it is an example—like the marriage ceremony of Petruchio and Kate—of Elizabethan nonchalance about dramatic time; but the sense could be that the guests *intend* to depart after the banquet, More having been called away.

As for speech prefixes, the one for More at Addition IV, line 182 seems to be unnecessary, and another should be supplied for the messenger at Addition V, line 2, although the marginal note "Mess T Goodal" would serve the purpose. There may be a

duplication of prefixes for More at line 1119, although an inter-
vening speech by the Lord Mayor could have been lost through
manuscript decay at the bottom of folio 15b.

These are very small matters: the dialogue and speech prefixes are as well arranged in this revised section as one is likely to
find in any Elizabethan dramatic text. The stage directions, however, contain seven clear errors. The entrance for More at Addition IV, line 1 is redundant once the soliloquy of Addition III is
in place. More enters for the soliloquy and then calls his man on
stage "Atired like him," but the "Enter Sr Thomas moore"
should have been crossed out. The same kind of error occurs at
line 878, where "Enter Sr. Thomas Moore" has been rendered
unnecessary by Addition V, which already has More onstage.
Four exit directions are missing: Addition IV, line 140; Addition
IV, line 181; Addition VI, line 55; Addition VI, line 67. An
entrance direction is required at Addition V, line 1. Hands B, C,
and E are represented in these revised scenes, with C doing the
majority of the writing as we have it. Once again it is clear that
while these writers were concerned with clarity in the flow of
episodes and accuracy in speech prefixes, they were willing to let
mistakes in stage directions pass for the moment.

The final section, beginning with scene x, concerns More's
downfall and death. Very few revisions occur here. Aside from
Tilney's objection to the scene in which More and the Bishop of
Rochester are required to subscribe certain undefined "articles"
(Tilney marked ll. 1247–1275 for excision, but the revisers did
nothing to repair the cut), only two important changes were
made to the original. Hand S revised his own final lines on folio
22a, showing that he was at least in part the composer as well as
the copyist of the text, and forty lines of the original text on folio
19a were marked for cuts and were meant to be replaced by
Addition I. Hand S's revisions are perfectly clear, but the relationship of Addition I to the indicated cuts on folio 19a has been
obscured by the one genuine mistake in the arrangement of the
manuscript as it has come down to us: the page containing Addition I was misplaced as folio 6. The correct position of this page

has now been made certain by a small masterpiece of scholarly close reading. Peter Blayney has actually studied the wormhole on folios 19, 20, 21, and 22, and has found that it matches the wormhole on the misplaced folio 6. Apparently folio 6 was once placed between 18 and 19, next to the indicated cuts, protruding a short way above the tops of the other leaves, where it was eaten by a woodworm working through from the back of the manuscript. The insect got away before it came to folio 18. I cannot think that a more precise discovery has ever been made in the Manuscript Students' Room of the British Library.[14]

With pages at one time properly arranged, this final section of the play repeats the pattern of errors we have noticed in the other two sections. The dialogue and speech prefixes are virtually free of error. At lines 1160–1175 references to "good morrow" would have to be changed, for Addition VI has shifted the council scene to night. The meaningless "fashis" at line 1847 is merely a scribal error for "fashion." There are passages one could wish clarified (ll. 1191–1213, 1373–1374), but their sense is graspable and they do not contain mistakes. The speech prefixes are perfect. Once again it is only among the stage directions that any accumulation of errors can be found: entrance or exit directions are missing at lines 1281, 1521, 1941, and 1986.

This pattern of evidence, with errors collecting around the stage directions and with the other elements of the text virtually free of mistakes, will allow us to determine the manuscript's position in the transmission of theatrical text. The next chapter will take up that issue. Here, for just a moment longer, I would like to keep the focus on the locations of the manuscript.

I offer a final example of the discrepency between the theatre

14. "*The Booke of Sir Thomas Moore* Re-examined", pp. 180–181. Even Blayney, however, thinks that the dovetailing of Addition I into the original was a little careless (p. 174). The cuts indicated on folio 19 are in two of More's speeches. Between the two passages marked for omission remains a four-line exchange between More and Catesby. Blayney thinks this passage was meant to be cut too, and that it was "careless" of the revisers to let it stand. I shall show in the next chapter, however, that once the purpose of the manuscript becomes clear, this is another case in which the revisers have done their job accurately.

and the Manuscript Students' Room. Let us recall the work done by Hands C and E at the end of Addition IV, where a scene was progressively lengthened: Hand C thought to end the scene at lines 203–204 by calling for the messenger who begins the next episode; he then crossed out the call for the messenger, wrote or copied some more dialogue, but upon trying to end the scene with "exit" found he had to cross that out as well. At that point Hand E took over with thirty more lines, whereupon the scene finally ends, and the next episode is free to begin.

Anyone who thinks about the business of rehearsing and staging a play will see what is going on in this progressive lengthening of the scene. To lengthen this scene is to defer the beginning of the next one, and when theatre people have to patch together such a deferral they are interested in gaining one thing: time. Why does time have to be gained? The most common reason in the modern theatre is to enable the stage to be set for the next scene. The most common reason in the Elizabethan theatre was to enable costume changes for actors who were doubling roles. As it happens, both motives seem to be involved in the example before us, as I shall explain later. For the moment, however, I am concerned with how scholars think, and in the annals of scholarship on *Sir Thomas More,* these practical matters of the theatre have been virtually unthinkable. No one else, as far as I know, has ever discussed the patching at the end of Addition IV with staging and casting in mind.

What *have* scholars thought about the ending of Addition IV? Many have thought nothing at all about it, for the assumption that the manuscript is unfinished and incoherent enables one to ignore the details of evidence freely. The two scholars on *More* who could never be accused of ignoring details of evidence, however, both accounted for the ending of Addition IV in a strange way. I refer to Greg and Blayney; my extensive debt for their shrewd observations (they are my most frequently cited sources) does not prevent me from wondering sometimes what they could possibly have had in mind. Both Greg and Blayney said that Hand E's thirty-line contribution to the ending of the scene in question was intended to fill up a blank half page.[15] In the fifty years that separate their comments, no scholar seems to have wondered why a professional playwright should have been called in to fill up a blank half page. Perhaps he wasn't called in. Perhaps he happened by, saw the blank half page sitting there, and (being the sort who can't stand blank half pages) filled it up. I rather suspect, however, that it is the scholar in the library who gets to thinking that blank pages exist to be filled with writing. People in the theatre would find the idea bizarre.

To think about the theatre seriously, one must regard it as a place where work was done with an interest in economy. The economy of the theatre has nothing to do with filling the blank half page. It has to do with actors, costumes, stage devices, time, money—to all of which considerations the written manuscript can be added as a necessary means of organization. The treasure preserved in the Manuscript Students' Room as untouchable was in the Elizabethan playhouse put to use by human hands— Hands A, B, C, D, E, and S, among others. The task of theatre historians is to insist, even as we work in the one place, that our habits of mind be trained on the other.

15. Greg, "The Handwritings of the Manuscript," in Pollard, ed., *Shakespeare's Hand in the Play of Sir Thomas More*, p. 46; Blayney, *"The Booke of Sir Thomas Moore* Re-examined," p. 175.

2

Parts for Actors: Casting the Play

Let us put considerations of the library aside, then, and try to think precisely about how manuscripts like *The Book of Sir Thomas More* were used in the theatre.[1] The Elizabethan playhouses generated a proliferation of text. Although paper was expensive and the companies operated under the same pressure for economy that affects most competitive industries, the process by which texts were transmitted from authors to stage performances was heavily marked with writing. The authors' original drafts, known as "foul papers," normally gave way to a fair copy which would be the basis for three additional kinds of text: the parts for the actors, and, for backstage management, the promptbook and the "plot."

Actors' parts would always have been required, and copying

1. The basic source for documents and interpretation remains W. W. Greg, *Dramatic Documents from the Elizabethan Playhouses*, 2 vols. (Oxford: Clarendon Press, 1931). Alleyn's part for *Orlando Furioso* is printed and studied in Greg, *Two Elizabethan Stage Abridgements: "The Battle of Alcazar" and "Orlando Furioso"* (Oxford: Malone Society, 1922).

them must have been one of the largest tasks of play production.[2] Each actor received a written "roll" of paper which isolated his lines and gave the cue for each of his speeches. Thus the original authorial text was segmented into many texts, and these segments, the rolls, were used by the actors for memorizing and rehearsing. The textual basis for the performed play—the writing that lies most directly behind the performance—must be understood, then, as the actors' parts, and it is a huge disadvantage that virtually all these Elizabethan rolls have disappeared.

The promptbook and the "plot" formed a different category of text. They served backstage purposes and were useful in regulating the performance. The promptbook was followed by the bookkeeper, who would have noted marginally any special calls for properties or actors, and who would prompt when an actor dried up. At moments when the basic text of the actors' parts was forgotten, or misremembered, in other words, the text of the promptbook would fill the need. The "plot" was a one-page outline of character entrances (and, to a lesser extent, exits) which also named the actors assigned to many of the roles. It appears to have been hung up near the stage entrances as a guide to the traffic of the performance.

The most important of these documents for historical purposes would be the actors' parts, if a representative number remained. The point at which the authorial manuscript is segmented into copies is the point at which the theatre overtakes writing and turns to play. The parts are the essential textual medium for staging a play, the medium without which an authorial manuscript would remain unperformed, and the medi-

---

2. Preparing the parts would have been related to casting and doubling decisions, of which we know very little. As Gerald Eades Bentley says in *The Profession of Player in Shakespeare's Time* (Princeton: Princeton Univ. Press, 1984), p. 41, we know neither who was in charge of the casting nor what negotiations were necessary with the writers on this question. Later, p. 84, Bentley imagines that the players would have cast the major roles "in conference," and that the prompter was left to deal with assigning the minor roles.

um without which the plot and promptbook would stand as backstage guides to a performance incapable of occurring.

Moreover, the parts were the medium in which some of the obscurity and the clarity of Elizabethan dramatic texts must have taken hold. Edward Alleyn's part for the title role in Robert Greene's *Orlando Furioso* shows that the scribe was prone to error in copying from the authorial text and that he sometimes left blanks where he was uncertain of the original. One can imagine a scribe, in a careless moment, turning some obvious phrase into an incomprehensible "dram of eale," or one can imagine him leaving a blank at the same point in hopes that Burbage would know what the thing meant, or would ask Shakespeare. Alleyn's part also shows the actor filling in blanks and making corrections himself—where the scribe left a blank, Burbage might have written "dram of eale," having recognized a subtle meaning in the phrase that has not filtered through to Shakespearean scholars. All texts were copied into parts, in other words, and all texts were liable to change in the process of being copied, memorized, or rehearsed.

Yet in studies of Elizabethan texts, hardly anyone thinks about actors' parts. It is the promptbook that is thought about, perhaps because there are between fifteen and thirty Elizabethan manuscripts that might qualify as promptbooks, or perhaps because the very notion of a promptbook as something the company would finally assemble in reasonably tidy form and might even put on the shelf for future use appeals to scholars fond of neatness and libraries. Compared to the promptbook, the actor's part is almost as ephemeral as the staged performance to which it is essential. Indeed, all but one of the thousands of parts which must have been copied and studied in Elizabethan theatres have disappeared. The one part we have discussed—Alleyn's, for *Orlando*—is the only one extant from the Elizabethan playhouses.

That is why no one writes much about actors' parts. We must work with what we have, and what we have are other kinds of manuscripts. But there is no reason why actors' parts cannot be *thought* about—and it is the lack of thinking about them that needs to be corrected. To my knowledge, the only important attempt to think about actors' parts in modern textual theory is the hypothesis of "assembled texts" set forth some fifty years ago by Dover Wilson and R. Crompton Rhodes, who took their hint from Malone. The hypothesis involves complicated assumptions—a lost promptbook is supposed to have caused a scribe to assemble a new text, using the parts along with the theatrical plot—and after sensible objections from Chambers and Greg its effect waned.[3] The failure of one hypothesis, however, should not prevent our recognizing other possibilities about actors' parts in the transmission of a dramatic text.

We should try to understand at what point the parts were normally prepared. Until recently it has been assumed that the parts were copied from the promptbook as one of the final stages of theatrical transmission. A leading example should serve to show how confidently this untested assumption has been made. In his careful examination of the *Orlando Furioso* part, Greg was able to write: "Since A is an actor's part we may reasonably assume it to have been transcribed directly from a prompt-copy. So reasonable, indeed, is the assumption that, unless we find strong internal evidence to the contrary (which we do not), we are entitled to treat it as a fact."[4]

The assumption, however, seems to me entirely unreasonable. We must remember, as Greg often did, that the rapid production of new plays formed the commercial foundation of Elizabethan repertory companies. Philip Henslowe's records make it clear that plays often went into rehearsal while the authors were still completing the text or making final revisions. The only rea-

---

3. See J. Dover Wilson, "The Task of Heminge and Condell," in *Studies in the First Folio* (Oxford: Oxford Univ. Press, 1924), pp. 53–77, and his Cambridge editions of *Two Gentlemen of Verona, Merry Wives of Windsor,* and *Merchant of Venice.* Rebuttal appears in E. K. Chambers, *William Shakespeare: A Study of Facts and Problems* (Oxford: Clarendon Press, 1930), I, 153–155; Greg, *The Shakespeare First Folio* (Oxford: Clarendon Press, 1955), pp. 156–157. T. H. Howard-Hill, "Crane's Manuscript of *Barnavelt* as Promptbook," forthcoming in *Modern Philology,* usefully discusses the question of parts and will stimulate fresh thinking.

4. Greg, *Two Elizabethan Stage Abridgements,* p. 261.

sonable assumption about such a theatrical situation is that actors' parts were copied relatively early in the process, so that rehearsals could proceed; and that the promptbook was prepared later, to allow the incorporation of any additions, or revisions—or improvisations, for that matter—which rehearsals had proved either necessary or delightful.

Indeed, the extant correspondence from the dramatist Robert Daborne to Henslowe suggests that this was the procedure. As Daborne struggled with a play during the summer of 1613, he sent a flurry of notes to Henslowe, one of which shows that he was forced to rewrite portions already under study by the actors: "I have took extraordynary payns wth the end & altered one other scean in the third act which they have now in parts."[5] Greg had a notion of the significance of this statement when he said, in a footnote, "the preparation of Parts, therefore, sometimes began before the Book was complete," but he did not pursue the matter.[6]

Moreover, when Sir Henry Herbert was Master of the Revels he twice complained, in 1633, that the players already had their parts while he was still reviewing the book of a play for licensing.[7] The usual interpretation of this evidence, following from Greg, is that it points to an exception rather than the norm.[8] But there is no evidence so clear as Daborne's and Herbert's to establish a norm against which these supposed exceptions can be detected. This *is* the evidence, and although it is not substantial enough to declare any practice "normal," it does tell us that the parts were copied early more often than anything tells us they were copied late. Those who work in the theatre for a living may find it necessary, on occasion, to depart from the schedules of the ruling class. Are we really to suppose that the actors always submitted a finished promptbook to the Master of the Revels

5. W. W. Greg, ed., *Henslowe Papers* (London: A. H. Bullen, 1907), p. 73.
6. Greg, *Dramatic Documents: Commentary*, p. 198n.
7. Ibid., p. 193.
8. See, for example, E. A. J. Honigman, *The Stability of Shakespeare's Text* (London: Edward Arnold, 1965), pp. 19–20.

and then waited before getting started on rehearsals? In a theatre that depended on staging a new play about every two weeks,
I think the actors would have pressed ahead fairly often, with
their parts in hand. If this seems a matter of common sense, and
if the available evidence from Daborne and Herbert agrees with
it, one is hard pressed to see why the practice should be treated
as an exception.

I am following the lead of the one textual scholar who has, to
my knowledge, read the evidence properly. Fredson Bowers
thought that Daborne's letter pointed to a common practice in
the playhouse:

> no play is produced at present without a great deal of adjustment
> during rehearsal both in large and in small matters, and we have no
> right to assume that conditions were essentially different in the
> Elizabethan theatre. It would seem logical to suppose that the im-
> portant prompt book would reflect as closely as possible the form
> of the plays as altered and revised during the practical tests of
> rehearsal. If this is so, the reduction of the author's manuscript to
> prompt copy would be the final [textual] act of the play's produc-
> tion. . . . My own opinion is that the preparation of the parts would
> normally precede the prompt-copy transcription.[9]

I submit that *The Book of Sir Thomas More* fully supports this
opinion. In the copying of parts, a scribe would require exactly
those elements which have been finished in the manuscript: a
coherent text and accurate prefixes for the assignment of roles.
Those qualities the manuscript lacks—consistent legibility and
finished stage directions—would not create problems in the
copying of parts. To a scribe illegibility is an occupational haz-
ard, and entrance and exit directions are somewhat irrelevant to
his task. The extant part of *Orlando Furioso* has only four plain
entrance and exit directions, one of which was added by Alleyn,

9. Fredson Bowers, *On Editing Shakespeare and the Elizabethan Dramatists* (Philadelphia: Univ. of Pennsylvania Library, 1955), pp. 111–112. See also Howard-
Hill, "Crane's Manuscript of *Barnavelt* as Promptbook," which recognizes a distinction between the "book of the play," used for parts and other rehearsal
purposes, and the "promptbook," used to regulate performances.

and between three and seven such directions are missing.[10] Directions for stage business and gestures—"he walketh up & downe," "currunt"—occur in interesting profusion; but the scribe seems to have paid no consistent attention to entrances and exits, the exact pattern of such movements presumably being recorded on the backstage document devoted to the traffic of the actors, the "plot."

Although modern textual theory does not take the parts into account, they have been urged as the solution to a particular textual problem in Shakespeare studies. The Folio text of 2 Henry IV differs from the Quarto in ways that cannot be explained by the usual theories—that the Folio is based on a copy of the Quarto annotated with production details, or on a new transcript of the promptbook. Neither of these theories accounts for a peculiar kind of omission in the Folio, according to the play's recent editor, P. H. Davison, and that is exactly the kind of omission which occurs in the revised manuscript of Sir Thomas More: the omission of stage directions. Davison recognizes that actors' parts would be the textual medium in which stage directions might disappear. His solution—that a transcript was assembled from the parts and became the copy for the Folio text—does not seem to me as likely as the possibility that the parts were prepared from the manuscript, which had been edited for exactly that purpose, touched up in all ways that would matter for the actors in learning their lines, the one element unnecessary for that purpose being the one element that is missing in the Folio text, the stage directions. There are other Shakespearean textual puzzles susceptible to the same solution, I believe, but this is not the place to study them. I mention 2 Henry IV because one editor has seen that the missing stage directions can be explained by the real work of the theatre, the preparing of parts.[11]

10. Counted by comparison with the printed quarto directions. Three of Alleyn's entrance-exit directions are missing (ll. 119, 377, 421), as are four for other characters which could have been marked in his part.

11. See 2 Henry IV, ed. P. H. Davison (Harmondsworth: Penguin, 1977), pp. 287–296. The other textual theories are fairly represented in M. A. Shaaber,

Perhaps one of the examples of misunderstanding which we considered in the previous chapter will help to clarify the case of *More*. Addition I, it will be recalled, is a rewriting of speeches by More in the original scene xiii, folio 19a. Blayney's consideration of the revision, which is the most specific and detailed to date, convincingly shows that one purpose of the revision was to eliminate some lines about "the Prince, in all his sweet gorgde mawe" which could be taken as an offensive reference to Henry VIII.[12] The author is careful about politics, in other words, and Blayney also imagines him carefully measuring out the lines of his revision so that they will fit over the space of the original (he was trying to fill up the page again). Yet Blayney finds the job "careless" in leaving a four-line exchange between More and Catesby standing on folio 19a. But there is nothing careless here. Blayney is taking the manuscript as a book to be read rather than as a text to be copied. He assumes that the crossed-out part of folio 19a is to be replaced wholesale by the new page on which Addition I is written, and he supposes that the four-line exchange should be part of the wholesale cut. Imagine, instead, a scribe whose business it is to transcribe speeches for each actor. The scribe will disregard the original speech by More beginning at line 1471 and will copy instead the entire continuous speech which is Addition I. He will then set aside Addition I, will return to the original, find the next lines that have been left standing (which are the four-line exchange), copy them onto the appropriate parts, disregard the portion of More's speech marked for omission (ll. 1506 ff.), and resume copying with the next speech left intact, which is by a servant who enters with news.

The scribe, in other words, is following the revised text exactly. Once the speeches are copied and the actors have them in rehearsal, here is what will be said (assuming the *actors* make no

ed., New Variorum 2 *Henry IV* (Philadelphia: Lippincott, 1940); A. R. Humphries, ed., New Arden 2 *Henry IV* (London: Methuen, 1966); and Alice Walker, *Textual Problems of the First Folio* (Cambridge: Cambridge Univ. Press, 1953).

12. Peter Blayney, "*The Booke of Sir Thomas Moore* Re-examined," *Studies in Philology*, 69 (1972), 167–191.

errors) from the final lines of Addition I through to the servant's entrance:

More.	But you poor Gentlemen, that had no place
	T'enrich your selves but by loathed bribery
	Which I abhored, and never found you loved,
	Think, when an oak falls, underwood shrinks down
	And yet may live though bruis'd. I pray ye strive
	To shun my ruin, for the axe is set
	Even at my root to fell me to the ground.
	The best I can do to prefer you all
	With my mean store expect, for heaven can tell
	That More loves all his followers more than well.
Catesby.	Sir, we have seen far better days than these.
More.	I was the patron of those days, and know
	Those were but painted days, only for show.
	Then grieve not you to fall with him that gave them.

Enter a Servant

This is a modernization of what the revisers wrote. There are no errors and their text is ready for the copying of parts.

That parts were ready for copying implies that the casting had already been done, a point for which there is more evidence than has been realized before. The name "T Goodal" in the margin of folio 14a has been recognized as a sign that Thomas Goodale was to play the Messenger in Addition V.[13] The other sign of specific casting seems to have been overlooked. Addition VI, by Hand B, usually gives the proper fictional prefixes to the players' speeches: Wit, Vice, Luggins, and so on. But at line 61 and again at line 66, when it seems to be the Vice who is speaking, Hand B's prefixes read "clo," exactly the designation he used in building up the Clown's role in the earlier insurrection scenes. There is only one explanation for this. In the insurrection scenes, B clearly had a particular comic actor in mind as he created the new Clown's role; in composing Addition VI, he knew that the same comic was to double as one of the leading

13. Greg authenticated this marginal note, once suspected of forgery, in "'T. Goodal' in *Sir Thomas More*," *PMLA*, 46 (1931), 268–271.

players (the Vice is the obvious candidate), and the generic designation of "Clown" crept into two prefixes. Thus we have tolerable evidence that the revisers attended to the specific casting of the play as they worked.

Moreover, once one looks at the manuscript with the theatre in mind, the revisions performed by Hands B, C, and E have a deliberate casting design to them. The original version of the play calls for some sixty speaking parts, making it one of the largest of all Elizabethan plays. We shall consider the implications of the play's extraordinary size in the next chapter. For the moment, we may notice that the revised version rearranges the original text at exactly the points where the doubling of these roles would have been most difficult for the average Elizabethan company. This is not the only purpose behind the revisions (a purpose involving staging will be considered later, for example, and there is no reason why literary improvement cannot also occur when staging and casting are concerned), but it is, I think, the central purpose.

The bulk of the revisions have been inserted at two points in the original text. Addition II, consisting of five pages written in hands B, C, and D, has been inserted after folio 5b to replace an undetermined number of pages removed from the original. Hand D may have had purposes different from the other two writers, but Hands B and C were obviously cutting away at the profusion of speaking roles in the original text (even as a new role for a Clown was being built up). As for the other insertion point, the connected series of Additions III–V, which amount to about five pages of new writing, was inserted after folio 11b of the original (the insertion actually begins with a sheet pasted over the bottom half of 11b). The same two revisers, B and C, are at work here again, and again they seem to have casting difficulties in mind. This time, instead of cutting roles, they are combining two scenes from the original and are padding the action with extra bits of dialogue, in what I take to be a maneuver to allow time for players to double important roles that in the original text followed close upon one another. Then, after a return to the original text for an episode, comes Addition VI, which is also a bit of padding, a thirty-line supplement to the ending of scene ix. This time the writer is Hand E, making his only appearance in the manuscript, but the purpose seems to be the same, for the padding appears just before an influx of new characters.

Let us take Addition II first. Hand B's portion amounts to a copying of the original scene iv with nine speeches added for the Clown. Hand C then follows with the scene between More and the authorities, which in effect eliminates the original encounter between the apprentices and Sir John Munday and cuts Munday's part from the authorities' scene. As a result, four roles— three apprentices and Sir John Munday—disappear from the revised version. Their inclusion would have created a situation in which twenty-two speaking roles occurred in the first 500 lines of the play. This is an unusual demand in the drama of the 1590s, even among the larger chronicle plays and tragedies. Some examples are: 1 *Tamburlaine*, sixteen speaking roles in the first 500 lines; 2 *Tamburlaine*, eighteen; *Spanish Tragedy*, fourteen; *Edward II*, fourteen; 2 *Henry VI*, eighteen; *3 Henry VI*, eighteen; *Titus Andronicus*, fifteen. We will examine a complete set of these figures in the next chapter. For the moment, since the elimination of four speaking roles brings the revised version into line with the casting demands of other large plays, it seems likely that while Hand B was concerned to provide a new role for the Clown, Hand C was reducing the ambitions of the original text to the proportions of manageable casting.

Hand D's contribution to Addition II, on the other hand, seems to be free from these practical considerations. Indeed, as I will show in Chapter 7, his three pages may well have been part of the original text, now being incorporated in a later revision. Hand D's is the largest scene of the play, involving thirteen speaking roles, and although the manuscript shows that Hand C was concerned to allot D's speeches carefully among the insurgents, there is no clear sign that casting was a problem. It would seem that the elimination of four roles earlier in Addition II had solved the casting problem and that Hand C saw no need to alter the major scene of More's success with the mob.

The other package of inserted text, Additions III–VI, presents evidence of a different sort, but again casting seems to be the issue. First of all, the combining of two scenes from the original is a neat piece of theatrical economy. It entirely avoids a crowded episode in the original, which involved a riot in Paternoster Row.[14] How many characters were involved cannot be determined, because some of the original sheets have been removed, but the scene was obviously crowded. Six distinct characters carry the burden of dialogue in the sheets that remain (More, Shrewsbury, Surrey, Faulkner, Morris, Sheriff of London), and a reference to "the rest" at line 835 implies that the rival followers of Winchester and Ely, who engaged in the riot, were represented. The revisers, Hands B and C again, have preserved the main business of the episode, More's encounter with the long-haired ruffian Faulkner, by bringing Faulkner and some of the others to More's study and having them interrupt another humorous scene from the original, More's meeting with Erasmus. Gone is Paternoster Row and its rioters. There is no longer any crowd. Gone, too, is one of the major characters who originally appeared in Paternoster Row, the Earl of Shrewsbury. This may have been more important than cutting the crowd, for now the roles of Faulkner and Shrewsbury can be doubled. A crowd can be played by the tiring-house attendants if need be, but Faulkner requires an experienced actor to put the comedy across (with his silly "vow" about long hair, he is a parody of More's religious principles).

Additions III–VI also contain some padding that would relieve pressure on actors who must double roles. Addition III (Hand C) adds a soliloquy for More just before the combined Erasmus-Faulkner scene begins. The combined scene itself ends with the extension of thirty lines by Hand E, which is followed by

14. See the edition by Vittorio Gabrieli and Giorgio Melchiori (Bari: Adriatica, 1981) for sound treatment of this combination of scenes.

Addition V, in which B and C combine to build a little bridge to the next major episode and tidy up the Erasmus element of the plot by announcing that the learned man has gone home. Then, after the original players' scene, Hand B provides another extended ending (Addition VI), before the next influx of new characters. These have always been recognized as bits composed during the revision, but I do not believe that anyone has tried to say why they were composed or why they all occur in the middle portion of the play.

A glance at the play's structure suggests the explanation. Each of the three sections of the action involves a large number of characters who do not appear in the other portions. The situation can best be seen in a listing of those speaking roles of ten lines or more which do not carry over from one section to another. Each section has a large influx of new characters:

More's rise to power	More as Chancellor	More's fall
Lincoln	Erasmus	John Fisher
Betts	Faulkner	Lieutenant
Williamson	Morris	Catesby
Sherwin	Randall	Gough
Clown	4 Players	Butler
de Bard		Brewer
Caveler		Horsekeeper
Justice Suresby		Porter
Lifter		Hangman
Cholmley		
Doll Williamson		

As David M. Bevington has made clear, this is a situation typical of Elizabethan tragedies and chronicle plays, which in their linear structures always depended on doubling—sometimes heavy doubling—among some of the capable actors in a company.[15] *Sir Thomas More* is especially demanding in this way. Only three

15. D. M. Bevington, *From Mankind to Marlowe* (Cambridge: Harvard Univ. Press, 1962), pp. 170–262.

characters carry through the entire play (More, Surrey, Shrewsbury), and only six others of any importance occur in two of the
three sections (Lady More, Roper, Palmer, Lord Mayor, Sgt.
Downes, Sheriff). Even aside from the groups of walk-ons and
bit parts, which would add to the problem, we can be sure that
doubling was an important concern in the preparation of the
play for a cast.

Further, it is in the middle section—where the four additional
pieces of dialogue occur—that doubling problems would have
been most pronounced. Time for costume changes would have
been required at the beginning of the Chancellor section, when
some actors from the rise-to-power section would dress for new
roles, and again at the end of the Chancellor section, when some
would dress for new roles in the fall-from-power. Additions III
and VI occur at exactly these places. Addition III, taken together with the following dialogue between More and his servant, provides some forty-five lines involving two actors before
additional characters appear in the middle section. Addition VI,
together with the original ending of the players' scene, provides
over seventy lines among six characters before the final section
begins. Hand E's conclusion to the Faulkner scene, along with
the following Addition V, results in some sixty lines among four
actors just before the large players' scene. This point should be
clear: doubling is heavy in the play; doubling becomes especially
important in the middle section; the four pieces of new dialogue, composed during the revision and distributed at the
crucial points of the middle section, create time for doubling to
occur.

That does not mean the revisions were prompted by reasons
of casting alone. For one thing, we will see in the next chapter
that some of these additions seem to adjust the play for special
staging effects. For another, I have explained in the previous
chapter that Addition III contributes to the play's qualities of
plot and characterization, while Addition V helps to clarify the
flow of scenes. Even Hand E's thirty-line conclusion to Addition
IV adds a dramatic point in showing that Faulkner remains

unrepentant despite More's attempts at education. Without excluding such motives of plot and characterization, however, I
suggest that the pragmatic concerns of casting a large play offer
the clearest explanation for these four short pieces of revision.
The earlier elimination of the apprentice scene and Sir John
Munday suggests a similar motive, and along with the two clues
about specific casting for Goodale and the Clown, these points
indicate that the manuscript is a coherent theatrical document,
arranged for the personnel of a specific acting company, and
prepared for the copying of actors' parts. A scribe could prepare
the parts from the finished dialogue and speech prefixes of the
manuscript, and actors could play those parts with the additional
doubling time provided by some of the revisions.

Let us not lose track of the hypothesis that is taking shape
here. A package of writing was inserted into the original manuscript after folio 5b, just where the number of speaking characters is about to grow unusually large. Because one or more original pages were removed at this point, we are not certain how
many speaking characters would have emerged, but we can see
from what remains of the original text that the number was at
least twenty-two. The package of revisions eliminates four of
those characters, adds a Clown, producing nineteen speaking
characters where there once were twenty-two. Another package
of writing was inserted after folio 11b, where pressures of doubling would have been heavy in an Elizabethan company. The
hypothesis is that these packages of revision were inserted for
purposes of reducing an oversized play to more manageable
proportions. *When* this revision was made is not yet being addressed, but there is no reason to assume (as scholars have often
done) that the revisions belonged to the original production of
the play. They could have been done for a revival—and in
Chapter 4 I shall present evidence that some of the revisions
were made as much as a decade after the original play. Further,
there is no reason to assume that the three writers of the first
package, Hands B, C, and D, were working together on the
revision. As we have noticed, Hands B and C seem particularly

concerned over casting adjustments in both packages. Hand D, who writes three pages in the first package, makes no changes which seem to bear on casting and may not have been working as part of a team of revisers. His three pages could have been a separate piece of writing which Hands B and C incorporated into their revision.

To summarize, then, *The Book of Sir Thomas More* appears to be an authorial fair copy which has been heavily revised for specific theatrical contingencies and has been brought to the point where the actors' parts can be copied. That means, of course, that the play was at some point brought close to performance, either when it was originally written, or in a revival, or both. We do not know whether or not those parts were ever copied, but there is nothing in the playhouse evidence to suggest that they were not. If they were, and if the play was then rehearsed and performed, we should not be surprised to realize that all textual traces of the parts, the final promptbook, and the plot have disappeared. Nearly all of these things from the Elizabethan playhouses *have* disappeared, and the surprise is that one large piece has survived from the many *More* texts and parts that would have been written. That this piece was preserved as "The Book" of the play may mean that it was supposed to serve as the promptbook itself, or as a temporary copy from which a promptbook could eventually be copied. Modern readers have balked at assuming a prompter could do his job from such an untidy set of papers, but I cannot set much store by such primness. The manuscript has been carefully fitted together with the exception of the misplaced folio 6. Prompters were used to reading from manuscripts, and one of the extant manuscripts that is agreed to be a promptbook is written in the execrable hand of Thomas Heywood (who may also be Hand B of our manuscript). Anyone who can prompt a play from a Heywood manuscript must know his business very well indeed—I assume we are discussing persons who knew their business well—and although a prompter can hardly have found the *More* manuscript a source of professional pleasure during the production, I think he would have known how to follow along. He would not have found accurate entrance and exit directions in the manuscript, of course, but if our usual assumptions about the purpose of the "plot" are correct, he would not have looked to the promptbook for most of them anyhow.

I have avoided discussing Tilney's censorship in this chapter, because a clearer view of the purposes behind the revisions can be gained by concentrating on the procedures of the theatre itself before turning to the procedures of the theatre under state control. The censorship has been distracting to scholars. Before Greg, it was supposed that the revisions were an attempt to address Tilney's complaints, a notion which Greg firmly put to rest by noting that only collective insanity could have led a group of professional writers to address the censorship by rigorously ignoring it.[16] In the aftermath of Greg's edition, however, Tilney's complaints have continued to loom large in scholarly thinking, and now it is common to invent little fictions on the theme of "two submissions to the censor."[17] On his first reading, the fiction runs, Tilney had only mild reservations but asked for a second look. The revisions were then performed as though clear sailing lay ahead, whereupon Tilney took his second look and condemned the entire uprising section. There is no evidence for the two-submission theory at all (why would Tilney have overlooked the uprising problem at first?), and the evidence can be explained on other grounds.

What forces the two-submission theory into existence is the absence of Tilney's hand on any of the so-called Additional pages, the ones added to the original text. The absence of Tilney's hand must mean, according to this theory, that he did not see the Additional pages upon his first review. A second submission to Tilney is then invented on grounds that he would have wanted to see those revisions once they were finished.

16. Greg edition (Oxford: Malone Society, 1911), pp. xiii–xiv.
17. First propounded by R. C. Bald, "*The Booke of Sir Thomas More* and Its Problems," *Shakespeare Survey*, 2 (1949), 44–65. See also Blayney, "*The Booke of Sir Thomas Moore* Re-examined," pp. 170–177.

What has been overlooked is the absence of Tilney's hand on nearly all the *original* pages too. Greg identified Tilney's hand on only three of the original pages: folios 3a, 5a, and 17b.[18] The other deletions in the manuscript are either in the hands of the authors or cannot be identified. That Tilney omitted to mark fourteen pages of the Additions does not seem significant in view of his omitting to mark twenty-two pages of the original. Tilney's review seems to have been more vehement than thorough, and the absence of his hand is not good evidence for anything.

It seems far more likely that one review was enough for Tilney to determine that this play was dangerous and that the uprising scenes would have to be cut. Royal censors do not have to think twice about some things. He did not have to read far in the original manuscript to see that the small corrections he was making here and there (on fols. 3a and 5a) were beside the point. He then wrote his general condemnation of the insurrection scenes on the first page, perhaps glanced ahead to the politically sensitive episode where More is summoned for not subscribing to the King's "articles" (fol. 17b, the third marked by Tilney), and sent the manuscript back to the company from which it came. The only puzzle left for us to consider is why the revisers paid no attention to Tilney's political complaint but set to work on questions of casting instead. This is a puzzle only on the assumption that the revisions were carried out soon after the original text was written. There is no reason to make this assumption. The revisions, intended to improve the casting, could have been carried out years later, when Tilney's censorship could have ceased to matter because it was outdated.

We shall deal with this possibility more carefully in Chapter 4. For the moment, let me summarize by saying that real theatrical work seems evident in the manuscript that we have—and the real theatrical work performed by Hands B, C, and E was ap-

---

18. Greg edition, p. xiv. See also Bald, "*The Booke of Sir Thomas More* and Its Problems," p. 50. G. Melchiori, *Shakespeare Quarterly*, 37 (1986), 294 adds fol. 10.

plied to the points in the action where the pressures of casting would have been difficult. These writers were, I submit, revising the manuscript so that it would be ready for the copying of actors' parts. This stage in the transmission of text must have been regular in the Elizabethan playhouses, but modern textual theory has tended to ignore it. The identities of the authors of the play are not the primary consideration, nor is Tilney's censorship. The manuscript represents the work of the theatre, and that requires the attention of scholarship today.

3

The Original Play: Acting Company and Date

To think theatrically about an Elizabethan play—that is, to examine some of the opportunities and problems that would have required the attention of professionals who were putting together this play of *Sir Thomas More*—one must ask how many actors will be needed, what allowances for doubling need to be provided for the sake of casting, whether there is time for the doubling actors to change costumes, how many new costumes will be needed (conversely, how many old ones will do), if the technical demands of the major roles are within the scope of the company's leading actors, and whether the play is suitable for the physical stage the company intends to use. To the extent that we can recreate these considerations in accordance with the evidence that has come down to us from the Elizabethan playhouses, we are bringing the discipline of theatre history to bear on play texts. The one item in the above list which would change our work most decisively is the item about costumes. Plays must have been scaled according to the availability of costumes, and if we knew the costume inventories of each company in each year, we would be able to rewrite the history of the Elizabethan theatre.

In the absence of costume inventories (there are only two), we fall back upon the other questions, which concern casting, doubling, the technical scope of leading actors, and staging. *The Book of Sir Thomas More* is loaded with evidence about these questions, and most of it has been ignored in the voluminous scholarship on the play.

The original text of the play, for example, was designed for an unusually large company of actors (I disregard the possibility that it was a closet drama unintended for actual production—it has always been recognized as a manuscript connected in some way to the public playhouses). The size of its crowd scenes cannot be known, for there is no specific evidence as to what "others" would have become in production, but we can count the number of speaking roles in the original version down to the first lacuna, a stretch of action consisting of 472 lines and comprising four scenes along with the beginning of a fifth. Here are the speaking roles:

	i	*ii*	*iii*	*iv*	*Beg. v*
1.	de Bard				
2.	Lincoln			Lincoln	
3.	G. Betts			G. Betts	
4.	Caveler				
5.	Williamson			Williamson	
6.	Sherwin			Sherwin	
7.	Doll			Doll	
8.		Mayor			
9.		Suresby			
10.		Th. More			
11.		Lifter			
12.		Recorder			
13.		"Another"			
14.			Shrewsbury		
15.			Surrey		
16.			Palmer		
17.			Cholmley		
18.			Messenger		
19.					Harry

	i	*ii*	*iii*	*iv*	*Beg. v*
20.					Robin
21.					Kit
22.					(Sir J. Munday)

The list includes *all* individual speaking roles, no matter how small ("Another" in scene ii has only two words) in order to set forth the most obvious and unrefined evidence. The original text through the beginning of scene v, a fair copy written by Hand S, gives lines to twenty-one characters, and it is clear that a twenty-second, Sir John Munday, is soon to enter when the text breaks off at line 472. I have not counted the role of Smart in scene ii, who is named in the opening direction but does not speak. If Smart should be counted, our totals would rise by one (he would have required an actor, after all, but I am trying to keep the criteria for counting roles absolutely simple and consistent, and so "speaking roles" will have to do), and the point at hand would be even clearer.

The point at hand is that this is an extraordinary number of speaking characters for the opening scenes of an Elizabethan play. We know, of course, that the actors would have doubled some of these roles, but for the moment I am avoiding hypotheses about how the casting might have been distributed and looking instead at obvious facts, the fact of particular importance here being that *Sir Thomas More* requires an usually large number of speaking roles—a large number of costumes for distinct characters would be another way to put it—in the opening scenes.

I have counted the characters in the first 500 lines of every extant play assigned to a public-theatre company for the years 1580 to 1610 in the *Annals of English Drama* and have found that only twelve texts out of a total of 146 call for twenty or more speaking roles.[1] The original version of *More*, in other words, is

---

1. Alfred Harbage and Samuel Schoenbaum, *Annals of English Drama, 975–1700*, rev. ed. (London: Methuen, 1964). Included are all plays dated 1580–1610 inclusive and assigned, however speculatively, to one or more of the adult

in the largest 8 percent of Elizabethan texts when measured in this way. I am using the opening 500 lines as an index of each play's casting size, of course. One could count all speaking roles in all plays to be absolutely certain, but I believe the results would simply reinforce the point I am making with the index. *Sir Thomas More* has fifty-nine speaking parts in all. It is an extremely large play.

This strikes me as evidence for the vexed questions of dating the play and determining the company for which it was written. If the manuscript of *More* can be recognized as a document intended for real theatrical use, and if its authors have a claim on our attention as professional writers for the theatre, then the fact that *More* shares a leading production characteristic with only eleven other plays out of 146 should tempt us to pause over the evidence.

Here are the titles of the other plays with twenty or more speaking roles in the first 500 lines. Also listed are the year under which the title appears in the *Annals of English Drama* and the acting company to which the play is there assigned:[2]

---

acting companies. Plays whose company is "unknown" in the *Annals* are not included. All speaking roles have been counted, no matter how small. Substantially different texts of the same play (*1 Contention of York and Lancaster* and *2 Henry VI*, for example) have been counted separately on grounds that each text probably represents a separate performed version. With manuscript "plots" I have counted the characters named within the first 20 percent of the lines, omitting those attendant parts that are not singled out in any way. For example, in *2 Seven Deadly Sins*, I have omitted the attendants who enter with Ferrex and Porrex at l. 17, but have included the Warder who accompanies the Lieutenant of the Tower at l. 5 because he is singled out by function and was played by R. Pallant, who plays speaking roles elsewhere in this play, and I have included the single Servant at l. 11 because other characters enter "to him" and apparently converse with him. Text in W. W. Greg, *Dramatic Documents from the Elizabethan Playhouses: Reproductions and Transcripts* (Oxford: Clarendon Press, 1931).

2. I have made one addition to the attributions in the *Annals*. *Friar Bacon and Friar Bungay* is there attributed to Strange's men by 1592, but I feel that the title page attribution to the Queen's men must also be taken into account. I list both the Queen's and Strange's men, therefore, and here add a caution that the "Friar Bacon" which appears in Henslowe's *Diary* as part of the repertory of Strange's men may very well be the separate Friar Bacon play that goes under the title of *John of Bordeaux*. This matter is further discussed in my "Ownership of *The Jew of*

Title	Speaking Roles: First 500 Lines	Date and Company in Annals
2 Seven Deadly Sins	20	1585, Queen's; rev.1590 Strange's?
Famous Victories of Henry V	20	1586, Queen's
Friar Bacon and Friar Bungay	20	1589, Queen's; Strange's by 1592?
True Tragedy of Richard III	21	1591, Queen's
1 Contention of York and Lancaster	21	1591, Strange's? Pembroke's?
1 Henry VI	21	1592, Strange's
Massacre at Paris	20	1593, Strange's
Taming of the Shrew	20	1594, Sussex's? Chamberlain's?
Downfall of Huntington	23	1598, Admiral's
Sir John Oldcastle	23	1599, Admiral's
1 If you Know Not Me	22	1604, Queen Anne's

Two distinct clusters of large plays are apparent here. The first four titles are associated with the Queen's men between 1585 and 1591. When the Queen's men were formed in 1583, they were instantly the largest professional company in London: twelve leading adult actors, plus boys and hired men.[3] It is not surprising to learn that their plays demand an unusually large number of speaking roles. The other cluster consists of up to six titles associated with Strange's men in 1591–1594. Two of these appear in the Queen's group: 2 *Seven Deadly Sins* and *Friar Bacon and Friar Bungay* are thought by Harbage and Schoenbaum to have reached Strange's men in the early 1590s after being performed by the Queen's men (for a caution about the *Friar Bacon* assignment to Strange's, see note 2 above). In addition, Strange's men are listed as the originating company of *1 Henry VI*, of the version of *2 Henry VI* that was published in 1594 as *The First Part of the Contention*, and of *The Massacre at Paris*. Finally, *The Taming*

---

3. See my article "The Queen's Men and the London Theatre of 1583," forthcoming in *The Elizabethan Theatre*, vol. X.

of The Shrew, dated 1594, might be placed in this cluster, for the Chamberlain's men were newly constituted in that year by actors who go back to Strange's men and are named on the *Sins* plot.[4] These clusters do not seem accidental. Of all the plays assigned to adult companies between 1580 and 1610, only 8 percent run to twenty or more speaking parts on our index; yet 27 percent of all the extant plays assigned to the Queen's men in the *Annals of English Drama* and up to 37 percent of the extant plays assigned to Strange's men appear on the index. To put it another way, only three of the large plays (not including *More*) are assigned to companies *other* than the Queen's and Strange's men during this thirty-year period, and these three constitute only 3 percent of all titles assigned to the other companies. It appears that there were two extraordinarily large companies in Elizabethan London, neither with a very long career: the Queen's men in the 1580s, followed by Strange's men in the early 1590s.

This similarity between the Queen's men and Strange's men has not, as far as I know, been examined before. It now appears that Strange's organization of the early 1590s was formed to imitate and replace the Queen's men as the largest company, in a commercial effort to capitalize on the older organization's decline. Both companies were formed by amalgamation—they were meant to be the largest troupes. The Queen's men were created at a stroke by the royal decree that banded the leading actors from the existing companies in 1583 into a new troupe. The origin of a second large company some half-dozen years later cannot be determined so exactly, but it is clear that some time in the later 1580s or very early 1590s leading actors from the Admiral's men (who had startled and redefined the London theatre with their *Tamburlaine*) joined with other actors, some of them probably from the existing Strange's organization, some

---

4. For the date of the *Sins* plot, see my "Plots of *The Dead Man's Fortune* and *2 Seven Deadly Sins,*" *Studies in Bibliography,* 26 (1973), 235–244, which summarizes the arguments of Greg and Chambers on this point. For the constitution of the Chamberlain's men in 1594, see E. K. Chambers, *The Elizabethan Stage* (Oxford: Clarendon Press, 1923), II, 192–202.

probably from Leicester's men, to form an enlarged Lord Strange's men.[5]

The most noticable similarity between the two large companies is their sensational record at court. The Queen's men were intended to dominate the court calendar during the Christmas festivities, of course, and during their palmy days their performances before the Queen outnumbered the total of all the other public-theatre companies. Yet not even the Queen's troupe gave as many performances at court as Strange's men did in the Christmas season of 1591–1592, when they were called upon six times. By then the Queen's men had gone into permanent decline, at least in London, and the court record shows that Strange's men replaced them at once as the dominant company. During the three seasons beginning with the fall of 1591, Strange's men gave more court performances than the combined total of all other companies, thus repeating the hegemony established by the Queen's in the 1580s.

The question before us is whether one of these large companies can reasonably be connected to the original *Sir Thomas More*. Veterans of the *More* problem will know that the longstanding evidence of handwriting can be brought to bear on this question, but I beg leave to defer the paleographical evidence in favor of considering the theatre a little longer.

To say that the Queen's men and Strange's men were alike is to risk overlooking a major difference in their political implications. The Queen's men were a deliberately political company in origin, and their repertory appears to have followed the path no doubt pointed out for them by Sir Francis Walsingham. If one reads through the extant plays which carry the name of Queen's men on their title pages (in order to eliminate the more speculative assignments of plays to the company), one finds no conflict or disturbance that is not settled in the interests of Tudor conservatism. The political line of the plays is usually explicit

5. For a fuller account see E. K. Chambers, *William Shakespeare: A Study of Facts and Problems* (Oxford: Clarendon Press, 1930), I, 39–44.

and never in doubt. The Queen's men knew why they were created.[6] Lord Strange's men, originating (as far as we know) out of commercial interests rather than royal fiat, played a repertory of varied and unpredictable implications. Some of their plays are conservative in a stern, steel-ribbed, moralistic mode: *A Knack to Know a Knave*, for example, or *A Looking Glass for London and England*. This is not the political conservatism of the Queen's men. It is a moral and religious conservatism which in the aftermath of the Martin Marprelate uproar of the late 1580s would have seemed provocative and bold. It is, I think, the provocation rather than the conservatism that was characteristic of Lord Strange's men. My impression from reading their extant repertory is that Strange's men, while they performed all kinds of plays and were certainly not engaged (as the Queen's men were) in a deliberately political program, courted controversy and sensation more willingly than any other company of the 1580s and 1590s. Name the most sensational plays of the Elizabethan theatre: most of them will have been staged by Lord Strange's men at their London playhouse, the Rose. A reasonable list would include *The Massacre at Paris*, *The Spanish Tragedy*, *1 Henry VI*, and *The Jew of Malta*, all performed by Strange's men at the Rose during the seven months from June 1592 into January 1593. These are drastic plays—drastic in dramaturgy and in political boldness, for they seize on controversial subjects and vivify them with new techniques of stagecraft that could not help but draw crowds.[7]

I stress that contrast between the Queen's men and Strange's

6. The company is named on the title pages of *The Famous Victories of Henry V*, *The Troublesome Reign of John*, *The True Tragedy of Richard III*, *The Old Wives' Tale*, *Selimus*, *Friar Bacon*, *King Leire*, and *Clyomon and Clamydes*. Because of its references to Tarlton, *Three Lords and Three Ladies of London* can also be counted.

7. For Thomas Nashe's reference to the popularity of a Talbot play in 1592 (almost certainly *1 Henry VI*), see Chambers, *William Shakespeare*, II, 188. Gary Taylor has kindly shown me his as-yet unpublished article on "Shakespeare and Others: The Authorship of *Henry the Sixth, Part One*," which makes the most convincing case I have seen for connecting Shakespeare's play to Henslowe's title. The controversial nature of *The Massacre at Paris* is obvious, but Chambers, *Elizabethan Stage*, I, 323 has interesting information about the offense it was still causing in 1602.

men to prevent the mistake of thinking that the two companies came to prominence at Court along the same route. In origin and in repertory they were different organizations. Both, however, were large and dominating troupes, and the similarity that may have been most decisive for their control of the court calendar is that they both included the most famous actors of their day. The Queen's men were formed as an all-star troupe, although even in this assemblage of big names, Richard Tarlton became the leading actor of his time. The most famous actors immediately following Tarlton (he died in 1588) belonged to Strange's men. At one time or another during its brief career, the company included Richard Burbage, Will Kempe, Thomas Pope, John Heminges, Augustine Phillips, and George Bryan. But for public fame and the Queen's interest, the important thing is that Edward Alleyn came over from the Admiral's men. By 1590 Alleyn was the most famous tragic actor ever to have played in London, and now he was joining (or perhaps organizing) the newly enlarged Strange's men. Along with the experience and size of the company, in other words, along with the presence of a Burbage whose ability in serious roles would just have been making itself felt, or a Kempe whose fame as a comic was on the rise, Strange's men included the Roscius of his day, and that is why they were favored at court.

That brings us back to *Sir Thomas More* and its theatrical characteristics. Another unusual feature of the play has not been noticed before: the title role, which runs over 800 lines, is one of the longest in Elizabethan drama. I have surveyed the same 146 public-theatre texts from *The Annals of English Drama* to see how many other roles run over 800 lines, using the counts given for Shakespearean plays in Marvin Spevack's concordance, those given for some non-Shakespearean plays by T. W. Baldwin, and my own counts in all other cases.[8] Of the thousands of roles acted by Elizabethan players, I know of only twenty from the

8. Marvin Spevack, *A Complete and Systematic Concordance to the Works of William Shakespeare*, 9 vols. (Hildesheim: Georg Olms, 1968–1980). T. W. Baldwin, *On the Literary Genetics of Shakespeare's Plays, 1592–94* (Urbana: Univ. of Illinois Press, 1959).

Annals lists of plays assignable to adult companies, 1580–1610, which run to more than 800 lines. Besides More, they are:

Character and Play	Lines	Date and Company in Annals
Hieronimo, enlarged *Spanish Tragedy* of 1602	1018	1587, Strange's, Admiral's
Tamburlaine, *2 Tamburlaine*	877	1588, Admiral's
Barabas, *Jew of Malta*	1138	1589, Strange's
Richard III, *Richard III*	1145	1593, Strange's? Pembroke's?
Henry V, *Henry V*	1036	1599, Chamberlain's
Hamlet, *Hamlet*	1507	1601, Chamberlain's
Henry VIII, *When You See Me*	1018	1604, Prince Henry's
Duke, *Measure for Measure*	858	1604, King's
Malevole, *The Malcontent*	over 800	1604, King's and Revels
Iago, *Othello*	1094	1604, King's
Othello, *Othello*	879	1604, King's
Mosca, *Volpone*	over 900	1606, King's
Volpone, *Volpone*	over 800	1606, King's
Vindice, *Revenger's Tragedy*	over 900	1606, King's
Antony, *Antony and Cleopatra*	824	1607, King's
Coriolanus, *Coriolanus*	886	1608, King's
D'Amville, *The Atheist's Tragedy*	over 800	1609, King's (?)
Subtle, *The Alchemist*	over 900	1610, King's
Face, *The Alchemist*	over 900	1610, King's[9]

There are clusters on this list too. Nearly half the roles are by Shakespeare, for example. More than half come from the Chamberlain's/King's men of 1599–1610. What seems to me more revealing is the clustering by actor, for virtually the entire list can be divided between only two actors, the two who were the giants of their profession, Edward Alleyn and Richard Burbage. Alleyn was known to contemporaries for his performances as Tamburlaine and Barabas; he must have acted Hieronimo in the earlier version of *The Spanish Tragedy* at his father-in-law's theatre and thus is a likely candidate for playing the role as it was

9. *Timon of Athens,* not included on either list because it is not assigned to an acting company in the *Annals,* deserves special note as having a role of over 800 lines *and* having more than twenty speaking characters in the first 500 lines. *Timon* and *More* are the only (presumably) public-theatre plays, 1580–1610, which combine these characteristics.

enlarged sometime during or before 1602; and it was surely his return to the stage after 1600 that prompted the Admiral's men to produce such a star vehicle as *When You See Me You Know Me*, with its 1000-line leading role. (During the years of Alleyn's first retirement, 1597–1600, the new plays written for the Admiral's men had no role as large as 600 lines; the company's dramaturgy can be charted according to the presence or absence of Alleyn.) Burbage's contemporaries knew his performance as Richard III, Hamlet, Othello, Malevole, and Hieronimo, and it is clear that he played some of the other large roles that come from the King's men after the turn of the century.[10]

Indeed, for these years of 1580 to 1610, one is hard pressed to name any other actors who are known to have played such long parts. Clearly the King's men had one other, to join Burbage in the Iago-Othello and Mosca-Volpone pairings of 1604 and 1606, or the Subtle-Face pairing of 1610. Perhaps this was John Lowin, who was later remembered for his Volpone. Do we take seriously the gibe at Ben Jonson for having played a poor Hieronimo? If so, we have squeezed out a list of four players who are known to have taken the longest roles written by 1610—but with due respect for Lowin's talent, and with less than that for Jonson's, the list effectively consists of two names: Alleyn and Burbage.

Thus the two outstanding theatrical characteristics of the original *More* play—the length of its major role and the size of its implied cast—can be placed in contexts of similar characteristics drawn from all the extant public-theatre plays during the relevant period. The result would seem to be new evidence for dating the original *More* and determining its company. We must remember the limitations of evidence that attend all Elizabethan theatre history. With only about 20 percent of the plays extant, and with only fragments remaining from other kinds of playhouse documents, we face many blind spots. About Worcester's

---

10. Details about players' careers are drawn from Edwin Nungezer, *A Dictionary of Actors* (New Haven: Yale Univ. Press, 1929).

men in the later 1580s, for example, with whom Alleyn apparently began his career, we know little beyond their capacities for occasional rowdiness. Nevertheless, among the companies for which evidence is available, some discriminations can be made in regard to the original *More* play. The Queen's men, for example, one of the companies large enough to undertake casting demands like those of *More*, have left no sign among their extant plays of having an actor capable of the largest Elizabethan parts. We may suspect that they had such an actor (John Bentley, perhaps, or William Knell), but they have left no sign. The Chamberlain's/King's men of 1599–1610 (and later, one would assume) obviously had actors capable of the largest roles, but there is no sign that their plays were scaled up to the extraordinary casting scope of *More*.

Where the two contexts of evidence come together is with Strange's men of the early 1590s, the company associated with up to six of the extraordinarily large plays and the company that at one time or another had both the great actors: Alleyn was their leader, and Burbage is assigned a major role on the plot of *Seven Deadly Sins*. The ample resources which are envisioned by the composers of the original play belong, so far as the evidence shows, only to Strange's men among the adult companies acting in London between 1580 and 1610.

This evidence does not, of course, amount to proof. Any acting company might have bolstered its numbers on occasion to perform extremely large plays, and there must have been actors other than Alleyn, Burbage, and Lowin who could work up an 800-line role if they had the opportunity. We have no rule that says these things did not happen. We have only the facts that have become apparent under a method not used before, and the facts indicate that Strange's men were the Elizabethan company that combined the unusual theatrical characteristics called for by *Sir Thomas More*. This indication can be turned to a conclusion only if it agrees with indications derived from other methods, and that is provided by the evidence we have postponed until now, the evidence of handwriting. Largely on paleographical grounds, Strange's men have long been suspected of a link with *Sir Thomas More*. Pollard's influential essay of 1923, which is still useful today, looked to Strange's no less confidently than do many recent writers on the subject.[11] The basic evidence until now has largely concerned authorship and handwriting. Hand C, evident in many parts of *More*, also wrote the "plot" of 2 *Seven Deadly Sins*, which Greg and Chambers connected to the Strange's men of 1590–1591.[12] Among the actors named on the "plot" is Thomas Goodale, who is also named by Hand C in the *More* manuscript. Another play in Munday's hand, *John a Kent and John a Cumber*, was once bound with the *More* manuscript.[13] It bears a date of either 1590 or 1596, and has often been identified with a play called *The Wiseman of Westchester*, which the Admiral's men performed at the Rose after the reorganization of the companies in 1594. Not all these points are as secure as one could wish. The identification of *John a Kent* with *The Wiseman of Westchester* seems

11. Pollard's essay is the introduction to *Shakespeare's Hand in the Play of Sir Thomas More* (Cambridge: Cambridge Univ. Press, 1923). The most recent essays that point in this direction, by Giorgio Melchiori, William Long, and John Velz, are not yet published. They were prepared for a 1983 Shakespeare Association of America seminar on *Sir Thomas More*. I am indebted to the authors and to Trevor Howard-Hill, who chaired the seminar, for making the essays available. John Velz's argument does not focus specifically on Strange's men, but the parallels he cites between *More* and 2 *Henry VI* imply an early date and the connection with Strange's. Others who attribute the original play to Strange's men or who date it in the period of civil disturbances of 1592–1593 include Peter Blayney, "*The Booke of Sir Thomas Moore* Re-examined," *Studies in Philology*, 69 (1972), 167–191; I. A. Shapiro, "The Significance of a Date," *Shakespeare Survey*, 8 (1955), 100–105; Karl P. Wentersdorf, "The Date of the Additions in *The Booke of Sir Thomas More*," *Shakespeare Jahrbuch* (West), 1965, 305–325. See also S. A. Tannenbaum, *The Book of Sir Thomas Moore* (New York: privately printed, 1927), pp. 33–94.

12. Greg, *Dramatic Documents: Commentary*, pp. 16–19; Chambers, *William Shakespeare*, I, 48–52.

13. See Shapiro, "The Significance of a Date," pp. 100–105, along with E. M. Thompson's study of Munday's handwriting, "The Autograph Manuscripts of Anthony Munday," *Transactions of the Bibliographical Society*, 14 (1915–1917), 325–353. R. C. Bald, "*The Booke of Sir Thomas More* and Its Problems," *Shakespeare Survey*, 2 (1949), 44–65, gives a useful summary of evidence.

especially uncertain,[14] and even the attribution of 2 *Seven Deadly Sins* to Strange's men of 1590–1591, which has almost hardened into fact (and upon which much of the theatre history of the 1590s is centered), does not stand on a bedrock of evidence. For my own part, I think the name of Goodale in the manuscript is a false lead to Strange's men and must refer to the later Admiral's men, as will be made clear in a later chapter.

Ȳet the older evidence, with its insecurities appreciated, does incline toward Strange's men, and the case is substantially strengthened by the theatrical characteristics we have examined. Strange's men were an exceptionally large company with at least one actor capable of playing an exceptionally large role. On theatrical characteristics alone, they seem to be the company for which the original *More* was written, and if that hypothesis allows long-standing evidence of handwriting and authorship to slip into place, so much the better.

Hypotheses exist to be tested. Can we put pressure on this one? About Strange's men much information is available which we have not considered. Does the broader range of information undercut the hypothesis we have developed? The day-to-day repertory of Strange's men, for example, is recorded in the *Diary* of Philip Henslowe, who owned the Rose playhouse on the Bankside.[15] *Sir Thomas More* is not mentioned. There is good reason not to expect it, for Tilney's censorship probably kept the original play from the stage in the first place, but our hypothesis is that *More* was intended for a repertory which is known in detail, and we should inquire whether or not the known repertory can reasonably be thought to have been the intended place of this play.

The repertory is marked by an emphasis on English themes. Nearly 40 percent of the 105 performances during the steady run of February to June 1592 consisted of plays on English

14. See Roslyn L. Knutson, "Play Identifications," *Huntington Library Quarterly*, 47 (1984), 1–11.

15. *Henslowe's Diary*, ed. R. A. Foakes and R. T. Rickert (Cambridge: Cambridge Univ. Press, 1961), pp. 16–20.

history, romance, or fantasy. The most notable of these was the new play on Henry VI which we take to be Shakespeare's *1 Henry VI*, but we would miss the range and incoherence of the company's Anglicism if we thought that the political realism of the *Henry VI* plays was the only mark of their style. Boldness and innovation may have been the company's penchant, but they did not try to unify a style. *A Knack to Know a Knave* is about an English king too, and so, in all likelihood, was the now-lost *Brandimer*. (I follow Greg on the topics of the lost plays.[16]) If the *Four Plays in One* of this season can be taken as the *Seven Deadly Sins* play for which the "plot" is extant, the company was doing another Henry VI play, this one cast in the form of old-fashioned morality. *Harry of Cornwall* and *Sir John Mandeville* must have presented English episodes or characters; *Friar Bacon* certainly did, whether it was the play we know as *John of Bordeaux*, or Greene's *Friar Bacon and Friar Bungay*. *A Looking Glass for London and England* takes its angry lessons from Ninevah and brings them home to London. *Sir Thomas More* is like these other English plays only in regard to its Englishness, but that is the only way they are like one another anyhow. The English gallimaufry at the Rose suggests that Londoners were attracted to the theatre by an awfully variegated nationalism.

Yet there is another way of thinking about *Sir Thomas More* and the repertory at the Rose—a way that has been followed before, although I believe the evidence can be used more precisely than it has been. *More* was originally a dangerous play. The censorship tells us that. The period when it could have been written for Strange's men at the Rose was a dangerous time, and the danger was virtually identical to the episodes that were censored in the original play. In 1592 London was threatened with violence. A riot of apprentices actually broke out on 11 June, and its assembly point was at a play in Southwark. The immediate cause of the riot was offensive behavior by the police—the Knight Marshal's men broke in upon the family of a feltmon-

---

16. *Henslowe's Diary*, ed. W. W. Greg (London: A. H. Bullen, 1904), II, 148–157.

ger's servant with daggers drawn and carted him and some others to prison without charge—but the uprising had deeper roots, and it is the deeper roots that are revealed in *More*. Resentment against government authority stemmed from the anger against foreign craftsmen who had been streaming into London as refugees from religious persecution on the continent, arousing fear and anger among the English artisans in London. The government had been improvising allowances for the foreigners to produce and sell their goods, and the problem had come to a crisis in the weeks before the riot of 11 June.[17] Ambassadorial influence was being brought to bear on the Queen, who was urged to guarantee the safety and right to work of the foreigners. The Privy Council reacted to pressure from both sides. On 2 June they agreed to delay all "proceedings" against the foreigners, but also set in motion a secret inquiry into the number and dwelling-places of the "strangers."[18] The census was to be conducted in secret for fear of emboldening the English artisans and apprentices to take overt action—the Ill May-Day uprising of 1517, which is dramatized in *More*, had not been forgotten. The apprentices' riot of 11 June over the behavior of the authorities was a sign of what could happen if the larger issue of anti-alien resentment were to take shape in the streets.

Eventually, by the following spring, the aliens were being openly threatened with an attack from apprentices and journeymen—"apprentices will rise to the number of 2336"—and the Privy Council ordered the apprehension and examination (and torture, if need be) of all persons suspected of fomenting the threat.[19] Among those to be arrested and tortured would be Thomas Kyd, whose *Spanish Tragedy* had drawn large crowds to the Rose in 1592. (Kyd was eventually charged with atheism, but he was investigated because of the anti-alien threats.) Kyd would manage to shift the burden of evidence to Christopher Marlowe,

17. *Acts of the Privy Council*, new series, Vol. 22 (1591–1592), 506.
18. Ibid., pp. 506–508.
19. Ibid., Vol. 24 (1593), 222.

whose *Jew of Malta* had been one of the hits at the Rose in 1592 and whose *Massacre at Paris* had opened there three months before Kyd's arrest. These writers would not be sought because they wrote sensational plays for the Rose, of course, but it cannot have escaped the notice of the authorities that the playhouses in Southwark had a number of connections with persons accused of disorder during the anti-alien troubles of 1592–1593.

As others writing on Strange's men have pointed out, it does not seem by chance alone that all the elements of the 1592 disturbances are dramatized in the uprising scenes of the original *Sir Thomas More*. The insurrection of Ill May-Day begins with anti-alien feeling among English craftsmen, it refers to ambassadorial protection being afforded the foreigners, it emphasizes the role of apprentices in the riot, and it twice dramatizes a conflict between the apprentices and authorities (Sir John Munday and the Sergeant at Arms) who seek to control them. These elements do not prove anything about date and company by themselves, of course, but as long as a date in the early 1590s stands on independent, theatrical evidence it would be a little naive to assume that such a point-by-point resemblance between the play and the events of 1592 occurred by accident.

This is to imply that Strange's men were ready to exploit a dangerous situation and that they were ready to risk the displeasure of the authorities. I would find this difficult to believe of some of the London companies, but not of Strange's men. The Queen's men, for example, cannot be called a dangerous organization in a political sense (although individual members were violent at times); and the Chamberlain's men formed in 1594, which included some members of Strange's men, seem to have been circumspect. (They were rewarded by being taken under the King's own patronage in 1603.) The one indication to the contrary is liable to be romanticized. The Chamberlain's men did play *Richard II* at the behest of the Essex faction just before the abortive uprising in 1601. Their motive was financial rather than political, as all the trial testimony makes clear, but they would have known that the story of Richard II carried a special political charge near the end of Elizabeth's reign. The most plausible interpretation is that the company was secure enough to do something risky for the money. There is no further evidence that they caused trouble to City or Crown, and Chambers's summation seems judicious: the Chamberlain's men toward the end of Elizabeth's reign "had practically become an official part of the royal household with a privileged and remunerative position, the preservation of which depended entirely on the avoidance of offence."[20]

Strange's men did not specialize in the avoidance of offense. In 1589, ordered to cease playing, they responded "in very Contemptuous manner" and played anyhow.[21] Some were jailed on that occasion. The riot of June 1592 began at a play in Southwark, and although this may not have been at the Rose (Henslowe lists no performance for the day in question) the connection between Southwark riots and Southwark theatres cannot have improved the respectability of the best-known company and the best-known playhouse in Southwark. When all theatres were closed by the authorities two weeks later, the Rose seems to have been kept closed longer than the others. That conclusion follows from Greg's and Chambers's dating of 1592 for a petition and reply that passed between Strange's men and the Privy Council.[22] Under any dating, the exchange shows that Strange's men had been relegated to three performances a week at the comparatively remote Newington Butts playhouse while the Rose stood empty, but the Greg-Chambers date of 1592 puts a nice edge on the evidence. Strange's men claimed that they had to play regularly in their accustomed playhouse in order to prepare for the approaching Christmas season at court. Their lordships on the Privy Council were being reminded, in other words, that they were dealing with the Queen's favorites, who had (if 1592 is right) given six command performances the previous winter.

20. Chambers, *William Shakespeare*, I, 67–68.
21. Chambers, *Elizabethan Stage*, IV, 305–306.
22. Ibid., p. 311. Chambers also mentions 1591 as an alternative possibility.

If that was their strategy, it did not exactly work. They did not reopen at the Rose until 29 December 1592, in the midst of their three-play schedule at court. Repertory companies do not seek such a coordination of opportunities—establishing a commercial repertory in an open-air theatre at the end of December while trying to hold their advantage at court by rehearsing before the Master of the Revels and performing before the Queen. One wonders if the great company did not falter a little. They never performed at court again. In 1593–1594 the only court performance by a commercial company was a final visit by the Queen's men, and by the following Christmas Strange's men had ceased to exist as a separate organization. These were, of course, hard years for all the companies, with the plague running especially high in London, but the sudden decline of Strange's men may have owed something to the special regard in which they were held by those responsible for maintaining order.

If one glances at their state of affairs in, say, late June 1593, by which time one of their leading playwrights had been tortured over suspicions of atheism and anti-alien libels, while another, charged with similar offenses, had been killed in a mysterious tavern brawl, one notices that the company had not managed to give thirty performances at the Rose during the previous twelve months. Their patron (who was probably very loyal to the Queen and the Protestant cause) had been the subject of strange rumors, one being that he would be the next king should a Catholic invasion succeed.[23] I am aware of overstating the case. Strange's men were not a band of outlaws. The plague may be the reason why they did not open at the Rose until 29 December. Rumors about Lord Strange may have had no bearing on his company's reputation. Overstating the case, however, seems to me more urgent than not stating it at all, and I do not believe this case has been stated. The bits and pieces of evidence suggest that Lord Strange's men and the Rose playhouse were, from the

---

23. *Calendar of State Papers Domestic: 1591–1594*, ed. M. A. E. Green (London: Longmans, 1867), pp. 39–42, 67–71, 234, 256–270, 533–548.

point of view of the authorities, different from most companies and most theatres, the difference being that they were better versed in trouble.

It is not difficult to believe that this company intended to stage a dangerous play like *Sir Thomas More*, nor is it inconceivable that the royal censor would not let them do so. We are still on the threshold, of course, looking over the evidence to see if anything discredits the hypothesis that Strange's men originated *Sir Thomas More*. On theatrical evidence alone, they appear to have been the company that possessed the unusual combination of resources reflected in the original *Sir Thomas More*, and what we can determine about the repertory and general character of the company does nothing to undercut that statement.

If it was Strange's men, the original play must have been written by mid-1594, when the company ceased to exist. They had been forced to tour during the bad plague year of 1593, and touring would have been difficult for an unusually large company. There is evidence that they divided into two troupes on the road in 1593. Their patron died in April 1594. By mid-1594 a major reshuffling of the London companies was complete, and the members of Strange's men, of great size, brief fame, an aura of sensationalism, and far-reaching influence, were distributed into the Chamberlain's men and the Admiral's men. Respectability lay ahead. After a profitable decade, these two companies were taken under royal patronage. The actors who once replaced the Queen's men as the dominant large company in London, even while they gave offense to the authorities, found themselves King's men and Prince's men in the end.

To be precisely speculative, I would say that *Sir Thomas More* was originally written for Strange's men between the summer of 1592 and the summer of 1593 and that the representation of the Ill May-Day uprising was intended to reflect the crisis over aliens that was troubling the City during those months. Tilney's strictures against those scenes were meant to keep such a provocation from reaching the theatre—particularly from reaching a theatre in Southwark, where one riot of apprentices had already originated. The long interruptions forced upon operations at the Rose for much of the remainder of 1592 and most of 1593 would explain why no effort was made, as far as we can see, to revise the play along the lines Tilney demanded. Such a revision would have been drastic in any event, and hardly worth undertaking when the company was being forced onto the road. If one company more than the others was likely to act dangerously from the point of view of the City authorities, in other words, it was the company that Marlowe and Kyd wrote for, the company that occupied the Rose, and in all likelihood the company that submitted an inflammatory play such as *Sir Thomas More* to the royal censor. Perhaps it is no wonder that their existence was brief.

4

The Revised Play: Acting Company and Date

In turning to the revision of the play, during which most of the so-called Additional pages were written, we must first clear away a misconception that has always burdened studies of the *More* problem. It has usually been thought that the original play and the revisions were written within a short period of time and that the substantial revisions were all composed together. A mistake about the paper of the Additions has led to the latter idea. The Additions were written at one time, according to this idea, because the pages all came from one consignment of paper. It is easier to lay this notion to rest than it is to explain how it arose. Even if the watermarks on the Additional pages were identical, we could not say that the paper came from one consignment, for the very concept of a consignment that passed in one bundle from manufacturer to a stationer's stall is a modern notion that does not recognize the conditions of shipping, shuffled batching, and shelf-life on which the trade was based.

At any rate, the watermarks on the Additional pages are not identical. They are all of the common "pot" variety, but the pots are different, with those on folios 9 and 12 being larger and having a different base from those on folios 6 and 16. My impression is that all four watermarks differ from one another, but to break up the assumption that the Additions were all written together, we need be concerned only with the obvious fact that the watermarks on folios 9 and 12 do not match those on folios 6 and 16.[1] (While this book was in proof, Giorgio Melchiori published his careful study of the paper and watermarks ["The Book of *Sir Thomas Moore:* A Chronology of Revision," *Shakespeare Quarterly*, 37 (1986), 291–308], confirming that the watermarks in the Additions differ in size. He also feels certain, as I argue in Chapter 7, that Hand D worked ahead of the other revisers. Yet Melchiori asserts that all revisions were accomplished within a few weeks of each other and soon after the original composition. His reasoning depends on interrelated hypotheses: that the original Guildhall scene was abandoned in revision, that D wrote with that cut in mind, that the Guildhall scene was then restored, that D's passage was left uncorrected and was also misunderstood by C, and that topical allusions to be described in the forthcoming Revels edition place the revisions close to the original writing. This assumes the writers were incompetent and requires a delicate linkage of hypotheses. I prefer to note that no direct evidence places Hand D's pages at the same time as the other revisions and none places the other revisions at the same time as the original.)

There is no reason to assume that the Additions all come from

1. For the Renaissance paper trade, see Dard Hunter, *Papermaking: The History and Technology of an Ancient Craft*, 2d ed. (New York: Knopf, 1974), and Allan Stevenson, *Observations on Paper as Evidence* (Lawrence: Univ. of Kansas Libraries, 1961). I have benefited from the advice of William Ingram on this matter. G. R. Proudfoot confirmed my observation that the watermarks are different and helped me understand how the notion that they were the same settled into place. Earlier scholars who apparently noted the differences in watermarks are W. W. Greg, *Dramatic Documents from the Elizabethan Playhouses: Commentary* (Oxford: Clarendon Press, 1931), which alludes to "two distinct makes of paper" in the Additions (p. 244), and Michael Hays, "Watermarks in the Manuscript of *Sir Thomas More* and a Possible Collation," *Shakespeare Quarterly*, 26 (1975), which alludes to "some slight difference among these pot watermarks" (p. 67).

one consignment of paper. As for the other assumption, that the Additions followed soon after the original version of the play, there is again no reason to think this way. While it is true that some Elizabethan plays were revised soon after they were originally composed, it is also true that more Elizabethan plays were revised some years after they were originally composed. Henslowe's *Diary* makes that clear, but so does common sense. Any play being revived after a gap of some years would have to be considered for revision because the acting company would have undergone changes of personnel. This consideration would have been especially important in Elizabethan repertory companies, which depended on intricate patterns of doubling. There is no reason, in other words, to assume that a set of revisions followed soon after an original version, and there is even some reason, if one must assume anything, to assume that revisions belonged to a later revival. But we do not need to assume anything. We need to begin with a blank slate and look to the theatre for the first points of evidence.

The revisions were primarily carried out by Hands C and B, with a nice patch of writing from Hand E. The contributions by Hands D and A are probably not revisions at all. D's part, at any rate, is more likely to have been part of the original, as I shall demonstrate in Chapter 7. Many purposes are likely to have guided the work of revision. A necessary narrative link is provided by Hands B and C in what is known as Addition V. The characterization of More grows a little deeper with Addition III, in Hand C. A neat piece of dramaturgy combines the Faulkner and Erasmus episodes, originally held separate, in Addition IV, by Hand C. The staging of the play is sharpened by Additions IV and VI, as we shall see in the next chapter. These other motives do not contradict or exclude what I take to be the primary motive that can be detected in most of the Additions written in Hands B, C, and E: the motive of easing the casting demands of an unusually large play.

We have noticed that the original version envisioned twenty-two speaking parts in the first 500 lines, an extremely large number of characters. In revision, Hand C cut the apprentice scene altogether and removed all traces of Sir John Munday, while Hand B added a part for the Clown. The elimination of the three apprentices and Sir John Munday, together with the addition of a role for the Clown, has the effect of reducing the opening 500-line section to nineteen speaking roles. This is still a large play, but the casting could have been managed by a normally constituted Elizabethan company. The revised text permits a test that is impossible for the original version with its lacunae: we can determine the minimum number of actors that would be required to play the speaking roles if all reasonable opportunities for doubling were taken. I specify speaking roles because we cannot be sure of numbers when the text calls for such walk-ons as "others," or "attendants." Thus we cannot take the full casting problem into consideration, but we can be precise about the speaking parts, which can be counted and distributed to a hypothetical minimum cast.

It must be understood that this is only a hypothesis. In addition to avoiding the nonspeaking parts, we have no evidence that minimum casting for the speaking parts was actually followed. Something like this exercise would have been performed in order to cast the play, and in performing the exercise one learns to respect the value of Hand E's additional patch of dialogue just before an influx of new characters, and the opportunity of doubling two important roles (Shrewsbury and Faulkner) which suddenly appears with the merging of the Erasmus and Faulkner episodes. These are the kinds of consideration that went into the planning of an Elizabethan production. But the minimum cast is not a statement of fact. It is an index of possibilities. It specifies the economical limit of casting—a limit for which the business of professional theatre would aim without necessarily attaining it.

Doubling possibilities are defined by one's sense of the impossible. It is impossible for doubling to occur among characters who appear onstage together, and it is so improbable that an exiting character could be doubled with an immediately entering character that I call this an impossibility too. Other studies of Elizabethan playhouse documents support this range of impossibilities but indicate that just about any other quick change was possible: there are numerous examples of costume changes covered by fewer than twenty-five lines of dialogue, with one example taking fewer than ten lines.[2]

The extant manuscript "plots" offer guidelines about the number of roles played by different types of actors. The lesser actors could play seven or eight small roles in one play; more important players were expected to do some doubling; the leading player—most of our evidence comes from the Admiral's men, where there was a leading player—did not usually double at all; and the boys doubled only rarely.

Following these guidelines, here is a minimum cast for the speaking parts in the revised *Sir Thomas More*. The asterisks mark the two quickest changes, which are each covered by twenty-two lines.

1. More
2. Shrewsbury   Faulkner
3. Surrey   Mess. (vii)   Porter (xv)
4. Lord Mayor   Horsekeeper (xv)   Officer (xvii)
5. Lincoln   Roper
6. Lifter   Clown (iv, vi, vii)   1 Player (Vice)   1 Warder
7. de Bard   Suresby   Mess. (iii)   Sgt. Downes   Officer (vii)   Mess.-Sergeant (ix)   Catesby
8. Betts   Erasmus   2 Player   2 Warder   Servant (xiii)
9. Caveler   Recorder   Mess. (v)   Crofts   3 Player   3 Warder   *Gough
10. Williamson   Morris   Bishop   Gent. Porter   Servant (xvi)   Hangman
11. Sherwin   4 Player   Lt. of Tower
12. Palmer   2 Officer (vii)   *Randall   Brewer (xv)   2 Sheriff

2. The basic source for evidence about casting is David Bevington, *From Mankind to Marlowe* (Cambridge: Harvard Univ. Press, 1962). See also a useful summary of evidence in Gary Taylor, "Three Studies in the Text of *Henry V*," in Stanley Wells and Gary Taylor, *Modernizing Shakespeare's Spelling* (Oxford: Oxford Univ. Press, 1979), pp. 72–84, along with David Bradley, *The Ignorant Elizabethan Author and Massinger's Believe as You List* (Sydney, Australia, 1977).

13. Cholmley   Sheriff   Clerk   Butler (xv)

14. Doll   Lady Vanity
15. Lady More
16. Mayoress   Poor Woman
17. Mistress Roper
18. Other Daughter

All but one of the speaking roles in the revised *More* can be played by thirteen men and five boys, with the briefest costume changes covered by over twenty lines of dialogue and most changes covered by upward of 100 lines. The one role not covered is that of "Another" in scene ii, which consists of two words and would require a fourteenth actor. I assume an extra would have covered here. The minimum group of eighteen for speaking roles could play many of the nonspeaking roles too, although the insurrection scenes would require supernumeraries. There is no reason why a company of twenty-two or twenty-three cannot perform the entire revised text including supernumerary parts. This is not a small company by Elizabethan standards, but neither is it an outstandingly large one.[3] In other words, the revisions remove one of the original play's leading characteristics. Padded here and rewritten there, the new version takes on the shape of normal casting, which has been turned somewhat toward the average Elizabethan play. At once our search becomes more difficult. The acting company responsible for the average play is hard to find.

We are not entirely in the dark, however. The role of the title character, exceptionally long in the original, does not seem to have been shortened at all in the revision. Addition III even provides a new soliloquy for More. We cannot compare the old and new roles exactly (the lacunae in the original make this impossible), but it is clear that both versions run to over 800 lines and belong to the exceptional range in the plays of the period.

3. For the size of acting companies, see Gerald Eades Bentley, *The Profession of Player in Shakespeare's Time* (Princeton: Princeton Univ. Press, 1984), pp. 25–146.

If the revised play was still intended as a star vehicle, we also know that a specialty role was being added for a comic actor and that both Hand B and Hand C designated this actor, in speech prefixes, as the "Clown." (Along with his obvious role in the revisions of the insurrection scenes, where the Clown is added as Betts's brother, note the prefixes for the Clown in Addition VI, l. 61 and l. 66, where Hand B must have had this comic actor in mind for the "Vice" of the play-within-the-play.)

Clown scenes, of course, are nothing new in Elizabethan drama. The generic designation is used by various writers throughout the period. I sometimes think that Heywood would not have written plays if he could not have written Clown scenes, and Heywood is usually taken as Hand B. We do know one further characteristic of the Clown in *More,* however, and that is his penchant for doing comic improvisations. One of the insurrection scenes in Addition II ends with the direction, probably by Hand C, "MANETT CLOWNE," and although Greg thought this a mistake (Malone Society edition, p. 71) its purpose is clear to frequenters of vaudeville and burlesque houses. The Clown stays on after the others leave and improvises his gags. (This is in effect another Addition, which has always been overlooked because it lacks a text.)

As far as I know, the phrase "Manet Clown" occurs only one other time in Elizabethan-Jacobean drama, and that is at the end of a scene in the manuscript "plot" of *1 Tamar Cam,* which dates from a production by the Admiral's men in 1602–1604.[4] In this case we cannot be certain that the phrase refers to a textless improvisation, because we have no text of the dialogue of *1 Tamar Cam* to begin with. We can, however, be reasonably certain an improvisation was intended, because we know who played the Clown. It was the famous comic actor John Singer, who was especially known for his improvisations. Henslowe once paid Singer five pounds for his "vallentarey," which has been misinterpreted as his "farewell performance." A "vallentarey" is

4. Printed in Greg, *Dramatic Documents: Reproductions and Transcripts.*

a "voluntary," and "voluntary" was the Elizabethan word for "improvisation." Henslowe was paying Singer for an improvised entertainment.[5]

The "Manet Clown" scene in *1 Tamar Cam* is positioned to accomplish what the Elizabethan monologue often accomplishes—it provides time for costume changes. Just before Singer's routine, the plot shows that three minor actors, Cartwright, Marbeck, and Parr, are dressed as noblemen, while a character called Diaphines is being played by Dick Juby. Immediately after Singer's routine, Cartwright, Parr, and Marbeck enter as attendants, and Juby then enters as a musician. The Elizabethan monologue allows actors to change costumes. It may also serve other purposes. Hamlet's seventh soliloquy, for example, "How all occasions do inform against me," which appears only in the Second Quarto text, and which allows a small group of actors to double the new speaking roles that enter the play in IV, iv and v, contributes something to the Second Quarto's meaning, but it also contributes something to the Second Quarto's backstage timing. Singer's "Manet Clown" episode probably got some laughs, but it also turned three noblemen into three attendants.

Since in one of its two occurrences, "Manet Clown" refers to Singer, I think we are obliged to consider the possibility, no matter how slight it may seem, that the other occurrence of the phrase also refers to him, or at least to his company. The need to be skeptical about this possibility is clear. There were "clowns" in nearly all Elizabethan-Jacobean companies, and we can be sure that they all inclined toward the odd piece of improvisation even when the bookkeeper did not write a signal for it. Cautiously, then, let us consider Singer and *Sir Thomas More*. If this slender thread does not lead to a bit of weaving, we will let it drop.

Singer was acting with the Admiral's men at the Fortune when the plot of *1 Tamar Cam* was prepared. Greg dates the plot after

---

5. E. K. Chambers misunderstood the word: *The Elizabethan Stage* (Oxford: Clarendon Press, 1923), II, 177. Greg got it right in *Dramatic Documents: Commentary*, p. 63.

January 1602, and we can be fairly certain that it cannot be later than March 1604, by which time Singer had probably left the company.[6] The Admiral's men—or Prince Henry's men, as they were called after 1603—in this period are well known to us from Henslowe's *Diary*, and a review of their activity enhances the possibility that they were undertaking a revision of *Sir Thomas More*. Edward Alleyn, who had retired from acting in 1597, had returned to the stage after the company moved to their new playhouse, the Fortune, in 1600. When Alleyn returned, so did a host of his old plays. The intention was to capitalize on his famous roles from the Strange's repertory of the early 1590s and the Admiral's from 1594 to 1597. So revivals were staged of *The Jew of Malta*, *The Spanish Tragedy*, *Doctor Faustus*, *Mahomet*, *The Blind Beggar of Alexandria*, *The Massacre at Paris*, *Tamar Cam*, *Friar Bacon*, and *Longshanks*. For a few years after 1600, the Fortune was something of a revival house.

It is impossible to call Sir Thomas More one of Alleyn's famous roles, of course, for we cannot be confident the play was ever performed in its original version. Yet there is a reason why the Admiral's men would have been interested in dusting off even an unheralded play on Sir Thomas More. The end of Elizabeth's reign and the beginning of James I's saw a wave of plays on the reign of Henry VIII. The Chamberlain's men put on their *Thomas Lord Cromwell* at this time, and the rather small number of new plays being written for the Admiral's men during their revival seasons included two on Cardinal Wolsey, by Henry Chettle and Anthony Munday, in 1601, and Samuel Rowley's long play on Henry VIII, *When You See Me You Know Me*, which must have been written for the company shortly after Henslowe's systematic records end in 1603.

Thus our clue about John Singer leads to Edward Alleyn and the Admiral's men at a time when they were reviving the star vehicles that Alleyn had played in the 1590s and were also en-

---

6. Greg, *Dramatic Documents: Commentary*, pp. 160–161. For the list of Prince Henry's men, dated 15 March 1604 and not including Singer, see Chambers, *Elizabethan Stage*, II, 177. Chambers supposes that Singer left by March 1603, but this is based on the mistaken understanding of "voluntary" discussed above.

gaged on new plays covering events in the reign of Henry VIII.
Sir Thomas More qualifies on both counts—what was probably
supposed to have been a vehicle for Alleyn in the 1590s turns
out to look like a new play on the reign of Henry VIII in the
early 1600s.

Perhaps handwriting and authorship may be admitted to the
argument at this point. It has long been known that three of the
most active writers for the Admiral's men during this period just
after 1600, usually working on collaborative ventures, and sometimes revising old plays, were Anthony Munday, Henry Chettle,
and Thomas Dekker, who are the three identities most confidently asserted for the Hands in the *More* manuscript (Hands S,
A, and E, respectively; Hands A and S, however, may have
worked only on the original version). Moreover, Thomas Heywood, who is the leading contender among paleographers for
Hand B of the manuscript, had been an actor and writer with
the Admiral's men in 1598–1600, had then become associated
with Worcester's men after the turn of the century, but had
returned to do some collaborative writing for the Admiral's
shortly before Henslowe's accounts come to an end in 1603 (he
wrote *The London Florentine* with Chettle for the Admiral's in
December 1602–January 1603). Of the six playhouse Hands
discernible in the manuscript, then, four are known to have
been associated with the Admiral's men after 1600. A fifth, the
writer known as Hand C, can fairly be added to the list if one
follows Foakes's and Rickert's dating of another piece of C's
writing for the Admiral's men, the plot of *Fortune's Tennis,* in
1602.[7] The only writer who cannot be connected to the Admiral's men after 1600 is Hand D.

At a time when four or five of the writers of the *More* manuscript were preparing plays for the company, in other words, the

7. *Henslowe's Diary,* ed. R. A. Foakes and R. T. Rickert (Cambridge: Cambridge Univ. Press, 1961), p. 331. See also Chambers, *The Elizabethan Stage,* IV,
14. Greg, *Dramatic Documents: Commentary,* p. 131, conjectures 1597–1598 for
Fortune's Tennis, but his reasoning is based on unproved suppositions about the
meaning of "Mr." in the plots. I am grateful for advice from Gary Taylor on this
point, although he does not agree that Hand C was writing for the Admiral's
men after 1600.

Admiral's men were banking on revivals of old plays written for Alleyn and new plays on Tudor history. The little clue about John Singer does lead to a company that can reasonably be connected to a revision of *Sir Thomas More*. The Admiral's men/Prince Henry's men seem to deserve further consideration in this regard.

One of their new plays on Tudor history is extant: *When You See Me You Know Me*, which was published in 1605 as performed by Prince Henry's men. Because the play is not mentioned in Henslowe's records for the company, it must have been performed after March 1603, when the *Diary* ceases to be a systematic account. It is dated 1604 in *The Annals of English Drama*. *Sir Thomas More* is not named in the *Diary* either, so if it belonged to the Admiral's/Prince's men, it too must date from after March 1603.

The two plays are remarkably similar in structure (no matter how different they are in political implications). Both divide their Tudor chronicle material into three sections, the first and third serving as an approach to Tudor state affairs and the middle taking the form of "gests" (the King of *When You See Me* disguises himself, mingles with the rabble, and intentionally lands in prison, in scenes no more beholden to fact than More's disguise-prank with Erasmus and his impromptu acting in the play-within-the play). The leading role in *When You See Me* runs to over 1000 lines, which like More's constitutes about one-third of the text, and it is a star vehicle. There is a major comic role for King Henry's Fool, Will Sommers.

The possible doubling patterns of these two plays are remarkably similar. The revised *More* is by far the larger play in the first place, with fifty-nine speaking roles compared to thirty-nine in *When You See Me*, but the striking thing is that both plays reduce to about the same company structure if all doubling possibilities are taken into account: twelve adults and five boys in *When You See Me*, compared to thirteen adults and five boys in the revised *More*. Here is a chart for *When You See Me*, for comparison with the earlier one for the revised *More:*

1. Henry VIII
2. Wolsey
3. Will Sommers
4. Compton
5. Brandon
6. Seymour
7. Bonwit   Patch   Constable   Porter   Cranmer
8. DeMayo   1 Watch   1 Prisoner   Rookesby   Dr.
   Tye   Emperor
9. Bonner   Prichall   2 Prisoner
10. Dudley   Dormouse   *1 Servant
11. Grey   2 Watch   *2 Servant
12. Gardner   Campeus   Black Will

13. Prince Edward
14. Queen Katherine   Countess of Salisbury
15. Young Dorset   1 Page   1 Lady
16. Young Browne   2 Lady   Queen Jane Seymour
17. Lady Mary

*Briefest changes: 14 lines.

In addition to *When You See Me*, the extant plays produced by the Admiral's/Prince's men in the period just after March 1603 are *1 Honest Whore* (1604), *2 Honest Whore* (1605), *The Whore of Babylon* (1606), and *The Roaring Girl* (1608). Analyzing these texts by the method that was applied to *More* and *When You See Me* shows that they all reduce to virtually the same minimum cast for speaking roles and to virtually the same division between roles for boy actors and roles for adults. I shall shift the burden of charts for these four plays to an appendix and here present the results in a table. (The question marks for *The Whore of Babylon* signify the difficulty of telling whether fairies were played by boys or men.)

	Total Speaking Roles	Minimum Cast	Adults	Boys
More, as revised	59	18	13	5
When You See Me	39	17	12	5
1 Honest Whore	31	15	11	4
2 Honest Whore	28	17–19	13	4–6
Whore of Babylon	31	17	?	?
The Roaring Girl	36	18	13	5

Let us be clear about what this evidence shows. It shows that there is nothing improbable about the hypothesis that *More* was written for the company that played the other five texts. It also suggests that the hypothesis is strong, for the further a hypothesis is tested without running into improbabilities, the more secure it becomes. But the evidence does not *prove* that *More* was reduced for the Admiral's men, because we lack similar studies of the other companies for which the play may have been revised. One purpose of this book, as I suggested in the Preface, is to highlight the need for theatrical studies of all Elizabethan-Jacobean companies. Only then will we be able to judge finally the resemblance in minimum casting which we have found between the revised *Sir Thomas More* and the known plays of the Admiral's/Prince's men. It may turn out that many plays from many companies reduce to the same size and structure under the minimum-casting method. In that case, we will be able to say nothing more about the present issue than I have just said: there is nothing improbable about the idea that *More* was revised for this company, which on other grounds seems to be the relevant company. If, however, discriminations could be made between the London companies in regard to size and structure, then we would have at hand major new evidence about many questions like the one we are studying here.

I am projecting a large-scale endeavor, and although one person might be able to undertake it with the help of a computer, there are so many questions of procedure and judgment involved that the method would best be worked out through the give-and-take of scholarly cooperation. I am far from having done the entire task myself. I have, however, been tempted to steal a glance at the other turn-of-the-century company which has at times been proposed for *Sir Thomas More*. Those who think that authorship and handwriting are the first considerations have tended to identify Hand D with Shakespeare. They have also tended, in recent years, to argue that the style of Hand D is like the style of Shakespeare at the turn of the century or later, when he was writing for the Chamberlain's/King's men.[8] As should be clear by now, I do not follow this approach myself. The comparison of Hand D with Shakespeare's handwriting suffers from the lack of any certain example of Shakespeare's handwriting in a dramatic manuscript, and the 150 lines by Hand D seems too small a sample on which to base stylistic comparisons with Shakespeare's printed plays from the turn of the century. Nevertheless, the Shakespearean possibility has been urged by responsible scholars who think that *Sir Thomas More* must (therefore) have been written or revised for Shakespeare's company at about the turn of the century, and although there is no evidence that Chettle, Heywood, Munday, or Hand C had any connection with that company, I have taken a glance at it anyhow.

My glance consists of performing the minimum-casting test on two texts from the Chamberlain's/King's men. One is *their* extant chronicle on Tudor history, *Thomas Lord Cromwell,* which is like *More* in having a large number of characters, many of them nonrecurring. The other text is probably their most famous, the Second Quarto of *Hamlet.* I wanted to set *Cromwell,* which has some of the abruptness associated with the so-called "bad quartos," next to a text which everyone regards as a full representation of its play, and that is the common opinion of the *Hamlet* Second Quarto.

The results are shown below, with charts for each play to be found in the appendix. It can be seen at a glance that Q2 *Hamlet* and *Thomas Lord Cromwell* reduce to approximately the same minimum cast, as well as approximately the same division be-

---

8. D. J. Lake, "The Date of the *Sir Thomas More* Additions by Dekker and Shakespeare," *Notes and Queries,* 222 (1977), 114–116; MacD. P. Jackson, "Linguistic Evidence for the Date of Shakespeare's Addition to *Sir Thomas More,*" *Notes and Queries,* 223 (1978), 154–156; Gary Taylor, "The Date and Auspices of the Additions to *Sir Thomas Moore,*" unpublished paper (I am grateful to the author and to Trevor Howard-Hill for providing this essay in advance of publication).

tween roles for boys and roles for men, and that these figures are distinctly smaller than those for the five known Admiral's/Prince's plays and the revised *Sir Thomas More:*

	Total Speaking Roles	Minimum Cast	Adults	Boys
Cromwell	43	12	10	2
Hamlet	30	12	9	3

The most surprising point of all will have to remain in the background here: that a full quarto like Q2 *Hamlet* reduces to such a small company as nine men and three boys ought to give pause to students of the Shakespearean texts, for everyone knows that texts reduced for small companies are supposed to be "bad" quartos, and that the "bad" *Hamlet* text is the First Quarto, not the Second. What everyone knows in Shakespeare studies is usually a good target for fresh thinking, however, and it can be announced here that the "bad" quarto of *Hamlet* actually requires a larger minimum cast for its speaking roles (ten men, three boys) than does the "good" quarto. Let us keep to our subject, however, and also keep the hypothetical nature of the minimum-casting method in mind. There is no evidence that any of these plays was actually performed by its minimum cast. The minimum is what a businesslike company would aim for, but there is no evidence that it was attained in these cases. We are looking at indexes of each play's casting possibilities, and nothing more.

The indexes do seem revealing, however. Five plays from the Admiral's/Prince's company at this time scale down to the same proportions as the revised *Sir Thomas More,* and our glance at the Chamberlain's/King's men shows that two widely different texts reduce to their own level, which is unexpectedly small and distinct from the level of the Admiral's/Prince's men. The likelihood that *More* was revised for the Admiral's/Prince's men is not getting any slighter.

Could we possibly be looking at the actual size of the Admiral's/Prince's men? One would like to know how closely the hypothetical index of minimum casting corresponds to historical fact. We do have one set of historical facts about the complete composition of the Admiral's/Prince's men in the period we are studying, and that is the document with which this chapter began, the one that has John Singer and his "Manet Clown" scene, the plot of *1 Tamar Cam*. The task of analyzing the overall company named on the plot has been performed by Foakes and Rickert in their edition of Henslowe's *Diary,* and I shall simply copy their outline.

Master actors
Mr Allen (Edward Alleyn)
Mr Burne, Bourne, Boorne (William Birde)
Mr Denygten (Thomas Downton)
Mr Jubie (Edward Juby)
Mr Charles (Charles Massey)
Mr Sam (Samuel Rowley)
Mr Singer (John Singer)
Mr Towne (Thomas Towne)

Adult actors
W. Cartwright (William Cartwright)
A. Jeffs (Anthony Jeffes)
H. Jeffs (Humphrey Jeffes)
W. Parr (William Parr)

Boy actors
Mr Denygten's little boy
Jack Grigerie (Jack Gregory)
Jeames (James)
Jack Jones
Dick Jubie (Richard Juby)
Tho. Parsons (Thomas Parsons)
George (George Somerset)

Supernumeraries, who appear only in the procession at the end
Ned Browne (Edward Browne)
Old Browne
Gibbs
Gedion (Gideon)
Rester
Tho: Rowley

Boy actors
  Little Will Barne
  Gils his boy (Giles's boy)
  Jeames (James)[9]

The plot shows how a company dealt with a big play, a play which, like *Sir Thomas More*, depended on crowd scenes. *1 Tamar Cam* ends with a procession of national types and the Admiral's men obviously called on every playhouse attendant they could find. These are the supernumeraries of the last two categories above. In a play like *Sir Thomas More*, they would have swollen the crowd scenes. On the other hand, the speaking roles in *1 Tamar Cam* were played by the actors named in the first three categories: master actors, adult actors, and boy actors. The question is, how closely does this historical list correspond with our hypothetical minimum-casting index for five plays plus *More*. Here is the comparison:

	Adults	Boys
Minimum casts, six plays	11–13	4–6
Actual cast, *1 Tamar Cam*	12	7

The differences do not seem great to me, and I venture to suggest that in presenting the minimum-casting hypothesis we are very close to the actual composition of the Admiral's/Prince's men soon after the turn of the century.

Let us draw together the elements of the hypothesis and see exactly what it is. Sometime after March 1603 (when Henslowe's systematic records cease), the Admiral's men decided to revise the old play on Sir Thomas More. This had originally been written for Strange's men when they were headed by Edward Alleyn, one of the few actors for whom long and dominating roles such as More's were written. Other plays from the old Strange's repertory were also being revived for Alleyn: *The Span-*

9. *Henslowe's Diary*, pp. 332–333.

ish Tragedy, The Massacre at Paris, 1 Tamar Cam among them. These, like *Sir Thomas More*, had passed from Strange's men to the Admiral's via one or more of the actors who had made the same transition. Alleyn may have owned all these plays himself—he certainly owned *The Massacre at Paris* and *Tamar Cam*.[10] The wave of revivals was intended to capitalize on Alleyn's return to the stage after the new Fortune was opened. Along with his famous plays, *Sir Thomas More* was undertaken because it dealt with a period of recent history, the period of Henry VIII, which it had become fashionable to dramatize during the final years of Elizabeth's reign and the early years of James's.

Some of the revisions were written by Thomas Dekker and (if Hand B can be identified with him) Thomas Heywood. They may have been helped by Henry Chettle, although the page in Chettle's hand may go back to the original of ten years earlier. The revision was supervised by a writer who for reasons beyond his control would pass into history by no name other than Hand C. He had once been with Strange's men himself, and (following the path of Alleyn) had joined the Admiral's men when the companies were reorganized; now, some ten years later, he was still with them. He was probably more important to the company than any other single writer, for the kind of copying and planning he performed was essential to the performance of any play.

The manuscript these writers revised was for the most part in the handwriting of Anthony Munday, who was also writing for the Admiral's men at this time. Munday did not write any of the revisions himself, unless passages copied by Hand C were first written by him. The original manuscript may also have been a collaborative effort, for Munday may have been copying other writers' work along with his own.

The revision, along with bits and pieces here and there, consisted of two major insertions. Original pages were removed after folio 5 and folio 11. A package of revised text was inserted

10. He sold them to the company in 1601–1602. See *Henslowe's Diary*, pp. 187, 205.

at each of these points. Possibly these packages included some pages of the original, but for the most part they consisted of new writing, writing which (whatever other good purposes it served) was intended to address the problems and opportunities of bringing a play ten years old up to date for the Admiral's men at the Fortune playhouse sometime after March 1603.

One of these practical considerations involved casting. The old play had been designed for an unusually large company, and the Admiral's men were not unusually large. Alleyn's part did not have to be cut, of course, but some other roles (such as the three apprentices and Sir John Munday in the uprising scenes) had to disappear, and opportunities for doubling other speaking parts had to be improved by padding the play at certain strategic points. The limits to aim for were well known from the revival of other old Strange's plays and from the new plays being written for the Admiral's men. What was being arranged for *1 Tamar Cam, When You See Me,* the two parts of *The Honest Whore, The Whore of Babylon,* or (we are perhaps running a little beyond *More's* date now) *The Roaring Girl* was exactly right for this big play. When the casting and doubling were arranged for twelve adults and five boys (and the tiring-house attendants and boxholders were held ready to swell the crowd scenes), *More* was brought into line with the others.

At the same time that cuts were made, the opportunity was seized to add a Clown's part in the uprising scenes for the company's famous comic, John Singer. He was also cast as the Vice in the scene of the visiting players, a part that he could enliven without changing the original text, and he was given a spot at the end of scene iv for one of his improvised routines (as had been done in the revival of *1 Tamar Cam*). Alleyn and Singer together—the tragedian and the clown, both of them old-timers, going back to the days of the Queen's men (Singer) and Strange's men (Alleyn)—surely this was the combination that would draw crowds away from the trendy group at the Globe, where Armin was too subtle by far as a replacement for Kemp, and Burbage was struggling to keep up with fancy writing by Jonson and Shakespeare. So some of the Admiral's men may have been thinking. Alleyn and Singer may have thought so themselves. Not all commercial analysis proves accurate.

I have omitted Hand A and Hand D from this account of the revision, because their contributions may have been involved in the original composition instead. With Hand A, it is impossible to tell. Chettle could have written the one page in his hand as easily in the early 1590s for Strange's men as in *circa* 1604 for the Admiral's men. As for Hand D, I shall argue in the final chapter that his pages preceded the revision and were part of the original composition of the play. For the moment, however, he can best be ignored.

This hypothesis cannot fully account for one piece of evidence. The actor Thomas Goodale is named marginally for the role of the Messenger in the second package of insertions. Goodale was with the earlier Strange's men and his name is often taken as a sign that the play was intended for that company. I cannot read the evidence that way. The name is clearly connected to revisions made by Hands C and B during what the present evidence indicates was a revision for the Admiral's men after March 1603. Goodale is not named in Henslowe's records for the Admiral's men down to March 1603, and he is not mentioned on the plot of *Tamar Cam*, which seems to require the entire resources of the company. It is, of course, possible that Goodale joined the Admiral's men after 1603, too late to be picked up in Henslowe's records or the plot but in time for the *More* revision. We know nothing about Goodale after 1599, so the possibilities are, at present, open. If he was with the Admiral's men after 1603, however, one would hope to find him on the extensive list of Prince Henry's men in 1610, which appears to name more than the sharers; but he is not there. He would have to have joined the Admiral's after March 1603 and left them (or died) by 1610—possibilities, of course, but not ample ones. To erase the problem with such speculations seems no more satisfactory than resorting to the suspicions of fifty years ago that the marginal "Goodal" was a forgery in the first place.[11] Dating the revision after 1603 for the Admiral's men does address the Goodale problem, but does not solve it.

On the other hand, one major problem does disappear on the assumption that the Admiral's men revived the play after Elizabeth's death. None of the writers of the manuscript shows signs of heeding the stern condition laid down by the Master of the Revels, Edmund Tilney: "Leave out . . . the insurrection wholly." On the older assumption that the revisions were performed soon after the original writing and in the face of recent censorship by Tilney, it cannot be understood why the writers were so nonchalant about their "peril" (Tilney's word) as to leave the insurrection standing and even to touch it up. According to the present argument, however, Tilney's censorship of the original version, submitted to him by Strange's men in the early 1590s, is well removed from the revision after 1603. The anti-alien disturbances that made the original play seem dangerous were no longer a riotous possibility. More significantly, the Office of the Revels had undergone a change of leadership in 1603. Early in the new reign, on 23 June 1603, Sir George Buc received a grant by patent of the reversion of the Master's office. A new commission for the office, issued on the same day, repeated the terms of the commission under which Tilney had operated since 1581, but replaced Tilney's name with Buc's. These documents cannot be taken to mean that Tilney was replaced by Buc in 1603. Tilney clearly continued to play some kind of supervisory role at the Revels office until 1610, and it appears likely that the authority of the Mastership was divided between him and Buc until then. Who was responsible for the licensing of plays after 1603 remains uncertain. Buc certainly licensed plays for the *press* after that became a function of the Revels office in 1606, and there is

11. See the debate between Tannenbaum and Greg in *PMLA*, 43 (1928), 767–768; *PMLA*, 44 (1929), 633–634; *PMLA*, 46 (1931), 268–271, plus Samuel A. Tannenbaum, *An Object Lesson in Shakespearean Research* (New York: privately printed, 1931).

evidence that he allowed *Jugurth, King of Numidia* for the stage in the early 1600s; but the exact division of authority between him and Tilney after 1603 cannot be determined. A change in the political climate occurred in 1603 in London—that much is certain; and it is also certain that a change in the Mastership of the Revels was in the offing at the same time, although the change may have been effected over a period of years.[12] A play that seemed dangerous a decade before may very well have seemed tame enough now, and it may be noted that an insurrection scene rather like that in *More* was incorporated in Chettle's *Hoffman*, written in 1602 apparently without fear of censorship.[13]

12. Chambers, *Elizabethan Stage*, I, 99, thought that Buc became acting Master in 1603. That Tilney continued in office after 1603 is argued by Mark Eccles, "Sir George Buc, Master of the Revels," *Thomas Lodge and Other Elizabethans*, ed. C. J. Sisson (Cambridge: Harvard Univ. Press, 1933), pp. 409–506, and W. R. Streitberger, "On Edmond Tyllney's Biography," *Review of English Studies*, 29 (1978), 11–35. In private communication T. H. Howard-Hill feels there are no sufficient grounds to put Buc in the Revels office before the end of 1605, and that he was dominant there from the end of 1606. In his unpublished paper on "The Date and Auspices of the Additions to *Sir Thomas Moore*" (see note 8), Gary Taylor argues for Buc's role in licensing plays and concludes as I do that the revisers were working on an old play which would pass scrutiny in the new regime. The major difference between Taylor's argument and mine concerns the acting company for which the revisions were done. Taylor assumes that Hand D was Shakespeare writing after the turn of the century; therefore, he speculates that the Chamberlain's men purchased the play from Henslowe or that Shakespeare did some writing after the turn of the century for the Admiral's men. As Taylor acknowledges, there is no evidence for either of these possibilities.

13. I owe this point to Carol A. Chillington, "Playwrights at Work: Henslowe's, Not Shakespeare's, *Book of Sir Thomas More*," *English Literary Renaissance*, 10 (1980), 439–479.

5

Staging the Play

The professional playwright knows the stage he is writing for. He also knows that the performed play will make a visual impression which is not contained by the literary text he writes, and if he is well versed in his craft he will see that visual aspect of his work in his mind's eye just as skillfully as he hears his dialogue as the speech of actors. These truisms apply to any theatre which employs playwrights. In the modern theatre, the pronoun "he" has to be changed to include women writers. For the Elizabethan theatre, which was an exclusively male operation, the pronoun still has to be changed—to "they," for most plays were written in a collaboration of males. *They* knew the stage they were writing for, these Elizabethan dramatists, and *they* saw the visual effect of their scenes as they worked—if they were good at their business.

The writers of *Sir Thomas More*, in my opinion, were good at their business, especially in the visual design of the play. The task of recovering that design, however, is no easier for this play than it is for most Elizabethan dramatic texts. Most Elizabethan dramatic texts were composed not to be privately read but to be used in the theatre, used by practitioners who knew the stage and could be trusted to understand the elements of an implied visual design. As a result, Elizabethan stage directions explain practically nothing. When it comes to describing space and movement—all that we call "blocking" in the modern theatre, for example—they are among the most reticent texts in all of drama. The theatre historian who wants to recreate the visual side of an Elizabethan play or an Elizabethan theatre must be a most patient reader, listening to the implications of the text without much explicit help, because the positive evidence that we would like to depend on for the sake of objectivity is largely missing.

In dealing with *Sir Thomas More*, however, we do have one helpfully explicit stage direction. The second scene of the original version, which was left unchanged in revision, begins with this: "An Arras is drawne, and behinde it (as in Sessions) sit the L. Maior, Justice Suresbie, and other Justices, Sheriffe Moore and the other Sherife sitting by, Smart is the Plaintife, Lifter the prisoner at the Barre" (ll. 104–106). Such "bar of justice" scenes are common in Elizabethan drama, but in this case we know that the properties required for a large and formal court scene were pre-set and revealed by the parting of a curtain. My procedure in this chapter will be to build upon that one piece of explicit evidence by listening to the staging implications of the rest of *Sir Thomas More*.

We know something about curtained scenes in Elizabethan theatres. No aspect of the stage has been more fully examined. The Red Bull repertory was analyzed by George Reynolds in a path-breaking monograph about fifty years ago, and this has now been joined by studies of the Globe, the Rose, the Swan drawing, and the theatre for the boy companies at St. Paul's, along with several broad examinations of all plays from one period regardless of playhouse.[1] I feel that something more

1. Individual theatres: Bernard Beckerman, *Shakespeare at the Globe: 1599–*

must be said of the Rose, as will be clear in the next chapter, but the main point is that real progress has been made in this work.

No longer does anyone believe the "inner-stage" theory, which held that the Elizabethan theatre contained a sort of prototype of the proscenium-arch stage, a curtained acting area located behind the platform and capable of being pre-set with scenery.[2] The curtained scene in *Sir Thomas More* was a leading piece of evidence for the inner-stage theory, but under the study of individual theatres, together with increased respect for such pictorial evidence of the public theatres as has come down to us,

---

1609 (New York: Macmillan, 1962); Herbert Berry, "The Playhouse in the Boar's Head Inn—Whitechapel," *The Elizabethan Theatre*, I, ed. David Galloway (Toronto: Macmillan, 1969), pp. 45–73; Berry, "The Boar's Head Again," *The Elizabethan Theatre*, III (Waterloo, Ont.: Archon, 1973), pp. 33–65; Berry, ed., *The First Public Playhouse* (Montreal: McGill-Queen's Univ. Press, 1979); Reavley Gair, *The Children of Paul's* (Cambridge: Cambridge Univ. Press, 1982); C. Walter Hodges, *The Globe Restored*, 2d ed. (London: Oxford Univ. Press, 1968); Hodges, *Shakespeare's Second Globe* (London: Oxford Univ. Press, 1973); Richard Hosley, "The Playhouses," in *The Revels History of Drama in English*, Vol. III, ed. J. Leeds Barroll et al. (London: Methuen, 1975); Hosley, "The Discovery Space in Shakespeare's Globe," *Shakespeare Survey*, 12 (1959), 35–46; Hosley, "The Gallery over the Stage in the Public Playhouse of Shakespeare's Time," *Shakespeare Quarterly*, 8 (1957), 16–31; Hosley, "Shakespeare's Use of a Gallery over the Stage," *Shakespeare Survey*, 10 (1957), 77–89; Hosley, "The Staging of Desdemona's Bed," *Shakespeare Quarterly*, 14 (1963), 57–65; A. M. Nagler, *Shakespeare's Stage* (New Haven: Yale Univ. Press, 1958); John Orrell, *The Quest for Shakespeare's Globe* (Cambridge: Cambridge Univ. Press, 1983); George F. Reynolds, *The Staging of Elizabethan Plays at the Red Bull Theater* (New York: Modern Language Association, 1940); Ernest L. Rhodes, *Henslowe's Rose: The Stage and Staging* (Lexington: Univ. of Kentucky Press, 1976); Irwin Smith, *Shakespeare's Blackfriars Playhouse* (New York: New York Univ. Press, 1964).

More generally: William A. Armstrong, "Actors and Theatres," *Shakespeare Survey*, 17 (1964), 191–204; Andrew Gurr, *The Shakespearean Stage*, 2d ed. (Cambridge: Cambridge Univ. Press, 1980); George Kernodle, *From Art to Theatre* (Chicago: Univ. of Chicago Press, 1944); T. J. King, *Shakespearean Staging 1599–1642* (Cambridge: Harvard Univ. Press, 1971); George F. Reynolds, "Some Principles of Elizabethan Staging," *Modern Philology*, 3 (1905), 69–97; Glynne Wickham, *Early English Stages*, 3 vols. to date (London: Routledge & Kegan Paul, 1959–).

2. A sampling of the inner-stage theory can be found in Ashley Thorndike, *Shakespeare's Theatre* (New York: Macmillan, 1916) and John Cranford Adams, *The Globe Playhouse: Its Design and Equipment*, 2d ed. (New York: Barnes and Noble, 1961).

leading pieces of evidence for the inner stage can now be seen as too fragmentary and isolated to indicate permanent features of the playhouses. The Swan drawing, which shows no curtained space at all, now seems reasonably congruent with the evidence of stage directions in the printed texts, and the current assumption is that explicit directions for curtained stage areas are to be taken as exceptions to normal staging. Normal staging, no matter whether the fictional location is interior, upstairs, at court, or in the woods, is now assumed to have been platform staging.

Yet curtained scenes like the one in *Sir Thomas More* still have to be explained. That they indicate special staging rather than normal staging does not make them disappear. The past generation of scholarship has advanced two broad possibilities for curtained scenes. Many of these scenes are brief tableaus, "discoveries" intended to make a sudden impact upon other characters as well as on the audience. The large entrance doors at the rear of the platform—especially a central entrance, when one existed—could have been used to reveal these brief displays.[3] Larger curtained scenes, especially those that imply substantial action and dialogue within the curtained space, seem unlikely to have been staged in a confined remote space, and there is some agreement among scholars that an ample curtained pavilion or enclosure, perhaps one that was set up for occasional plays, was probably employed for large scenes of this sort.[4] Our example from *Sir Thomas More* is of the larger variety. A crowded scene is revealed behind the curtains, and the characters are required to remain at the justice bar and seats for much of the action (150 lines, for the middle section at ll. 154–202 could move out of the enclosure).

3. See Beckerman, *Shakespeare at the Globe*, p. 70, Hosley, "Discovery Space in Shakespeare's Globe," and Reynolds, *Staging at the Red Bull*, pp. 109–111. At the Rose, Dekker's *Patient Grissell* spells out three entrances, one "in the midst" of the others.

4. See Reynolds, *Staging at the Red Bull*, pp. 132 ff.; Beckerman, *Shakespeare at the Globe*, pp. 75–86; Hodges, *The Globe Restored*, pp. 51–65; Nagler, *Shakespeare's Stage*, pp. 26–32, 45–46; Lawrence J. Ross, "The Use of a Fit-Up Booth in *Othello*," *Shakespeare Quarterly*, 12 (1961), 359–370. Richard Hosley (see the works cited in note 1) disagrees notably with this possibility.

If a large curtained space is explicitly referred to in one scene, we must recognize the likelihood that it was intended to figure elsewhere in the action, although no other stage directions call for its use. Theatre tends to use its prominent spaces, and it seems more reasonable to assume that the curtained space of scene ii figured in other scenes than to assume that all scenes other than scene ii managed to avoid it.

Scene ii is an interior scene which uses stage furniture to highlight a moment in More's career. There are five other interior scenes in the original version of the play which do the same thing: they center on More, and mark the stages of his career through attention to stage furniture. These are the Erasmus scene (viia), the entertainment for the Lord Mayor (ix), the council-chamber scene where More refuses to sign the King's articles (x), More's lamenting with his family in a humbly furnished room at home (xiii), and his final encounter with his family in a prison room of the Tower (xvi).[5] These interiors become both more frequent and more prominent as the action moves away from the public insurrection scenes and toward More's downfall and death, the sense of location in the play becoming private and withdrawn as a successful public career turns toward tragedy.

These six interior scenes all require stage furnishings, which would have been arranged, it seems reasonable to assume, in the curtained area of scene ii. But a more important point is that the text pays much attention to these properties, making the objects of the interior scenes momentarily distinct. The table in More's study, where the Erasmus episode occurs, is arranged for a formal display of the purse and mace symbolic of More's new authority. The chairs for the Lord Mayor's entourage in the reception scene are the objects of More's amused fussiness as he

5. There are other interiors—iii and xv—but More does not appear in them. They are "unlocalized" in the sense defined by Beckerman, *Shakespeare at the Globe*, pp. 64–69, and could easily be played on the platform. It is only the scenes involving More that focus on properties and imply repetition in staging.

breaks decorum to give the Mayor and his wife priority in seating arrangements (ll. 878–991), and the council table in the next scene prompts a meditation on public responsibility (ll. 1176–1182). In the lamenting scene, a marginal note specifies "lowe stooles" for More and his family, and More himself makes the point about humble seats:

> God morrowe good sonne Roper, sit good Madame,
> uppon an humble seate, the time so craves,
> rest your good hart on earth, the roofe of graves.
> you see the floore of greatnesse is uneven,
> the Cricket and high throane alike neere heaven.
> [ll. 1413–1417]

In the prison scene we would imagine that the low stools have been replaced by the barest furnishings, perhaps a few plain benches.

The visual contrasts among these scenes are deliberate and clear. One motif follows the decline of the family group—from the ceremony of the Lord Mayor's entertainment with its rich furnishings, to the lamenting scene with its humble seats, and then to the final gathering of the family in the bare furnishings of the prison scene. Another motif follows More through various public chambers—from the sessions court in scene ii, through the council chamber where he resigns, and again to the prison where the Chancellor of the state has become the state's captive.

These interior locations, with their contrasts in stage furnishings, give a visual delineation to the *de casibus* theme of the play. The objects change in accordance with More's disgrace, but the implied use of a curtained area retains a unity of theatrical place through the different interiors. The dramaturgy of the play amounts to drawing widely different qualities of More's life into one stage space to gain a repeated visual impression, an impression of withdrawal from the open range of the platform stage. More's achievement in the play is entirely personal, a retaining of spiritual intergrity in the condition of public disgrace, and as the interior scenes increase the sense of withdrawal in the action, they also give visual unity to the dramatization of More's personal consistency in the face of outward change.

That is one way in which the staging of the original play matters. There is another, which concerns More's public confrontations. The two major scenes—major in the concentration of the writing and in the amount of time devoted to them—are More's quelling of the May-Day insurrection and his speeches on the scaffold before his execution. These are the moments of public action which define the rise and fall pattern of the play, for it is at the end of the first that More is elevated to power and it is at the end of the second that his downfall leads to death. Between these two defining episodes come most of the interior scenes which seem to employ the curtained space. If we look closely, we will observe that some sort of theatrical structure—very possibly the same curtained space—figures in these two major scenes, the insurrection and the execution.

The execution scene involves a raised scaffold, and some details of this structure are clear from the dialogue. More climbs a ladder from the main stage to the scaffold at line 1915, and he is able to exit from the scaffold to the tiring-house when he is led to the block at the very end of the play. The latter point shows that the scaffold was adjoining the tiring-house facade rather than standing free on the platform. Moreover, the scaffold seems to have been in place at the start of the scene, for there is no hint that it was set up as part of the scene's opening business. A raised acting area, projecting from the tiring-house facade and probably remaining in place throughout the action, answers the staging requirements of this scene.

The earlier major scene—the quelling of the insurrection—now becomes especially intriguing. More's important speeches to the insurgents almost certainly would have been delivered from a raised area of some sort. One rarely quells a mob from any other position, especially on a stage. Various devices could easily have provided a raised position for More (a cart brought in by the mob, for example), but the matter cannot be dismissed without offering the possibility that More's speeches were delivered from exactly the same raised area which served as the scaffold in the final scene.

There is something more than guesswork to this possibility. What one notices, in comparing the insurrection scene with the execution scene, is a similarity in the grouping of characters. The Earls of Shrewsbury and Surrey are prominent figures with More at their entrance in the insurrection scene. In fact, as the mob argues over who should be heard, the dramatic point is that the two noblemen are rejected in favor of the apparently lesser figure of Sheriff More. Turning to the execution scene, we notice that as More climbs to the level of the scaffold, he there encounters the Earls of Shrewsbury and Surrey. It is clear that they are with More on the scaffold,[6] and the scene exactly reverses the dramatic sense of the insurrection scene: where before More moved into prominence from the company of Shrewsbury and Surrey, now he leaves them behind as he goes to his death. The similarity of character groupings is quite obvious; and I would go on to suggest that the scaffold staging of the final scene is a visual recollection of the raised area from which More, attended by Surrey and Shrewsbury, calmed the insurrection.

This is perhaps as far as the evidence of the manuscript goes toward revealing an intentional and coherent design in stagecraft. Visual repetition persists through the major interiors of the play, and visual similarity relates the public scenes of More's rise to power and his execution. We should not let matters rest,

6. The direction reads: "As he is going up the stayres, enters [sic] the Earles of Surrye & Shrewsburie" (l. 1920), and More's next speech indicates that once he reaches the level of the scaffold, Surrey and Shrewsbury are beside him ("The higher I mounte, the better I can see my friends about me"). In a paper soon to be published, Giorgio Melchiori disagrees with my view of the staging and prefers to locate Shrewsbury and Surrey on the lower level, More being thus more nearly isolated above for his "apotheosis." This requires reading "my friends about me" as "my friends below me"; it seems more likely that "about" means "surrounding" and within reach on the raised level.

however, without noticing which of the Elizabethan staging techniques discussed earlier would best serve for the evidence we have presented. A curtained pavilion or booth, projecting part way onto the platform, would afford space both for curtained interior scenes (at the platform level) and for raised scenes (at the roof level of the projecting enclosure). If such a pavilion were used for *Sir Thomas More,* the two kinds of visual recollection we have noticed in the play would belong to the figuration of a single physical structure. The raised area would hold the crucial public scenes, and the curtained area would contain the interiors; More's private and public moments would gain an insistent visual relation to one another.

Perhaps the text of the play will make this possibility clear. At the end of the play as he ascends the scaffold and prepares for death, More knows that he has achieved a spiritual integrity which raises him above the failure of his worldly career:

> There is a thing within me, that will raise
> and elevate my better parte bove sight
> of these same weaker eyes. And Mr. Shreeves,
> for all this troupe of steele that tends my death,
> I shall breake from you, and flye up to heaven,
> Lets seeke the meanes for this.

That spiritual achievement, which has been earlier dramatized in the series of interior scenes, is now rehearsed within the final scene itself. As More stands on a raised area, perhaps directly above the curtained area which has represented his law court (scene ii), his council chamber (scene x), his home (scenes ix and xii), and his prison (scene xvi), he touches on these locations of his career before expressing his sense of religious elevation. To the executioner he makes a conceit about a lawsuit, to Shrewsbury he summons himself as a stage player, again to the executioner he refers to an event in his prison, and walking across the scaffold he remembers his house at Chelsea. It is an alert moment in the theatre to bring into these final speeches a recollection of the locations of More's career; and on the hypothesis of a booth stage, those locations would have been represented within the structure which, at a raised and public level, he now crosses to his martyrdom.

This is sophisticated dramaturgy. The locations of More's career are figured through visual repetition, setting up a possibility of verbal recollection at the end which is realized in the hero's final lines. The lesser Elizabethan writers are not often thought to have done that kind of work. The lesser Elizabethan dramatists are usually thought of as hacks, and the writers of our manuscript include some lesser Elizabethan dramatists. Hand C is not even considered to have been a hack writer. He was a "scribe" or a "playhouse functionary." What helps to set such writers apart from the canonized dramatists is that they collaborated, collaborated to such an extent that their status as authors remained indistinct under the category of individual genius by which the literary canon was formed. The manuscript of *Sir Thomas More* has seemed the epitome of hack writing (apart from Hand D's pages, of course) because it has so very many collaborators. Lying at such a distance from individual genius and the literary canon, it was almost bound to be regarded as incoherent and unfinished. In arguing that the manuscript is, on the contrary, the product of sophisticated dramaturgy, I am offering a reminder that the theatre is a place of collaboration from the beginning to the end of its enterprise. Even Hand D collaborated—that is the first thing to be noticed about him.

If these hacks were sophisticated in dramaturgy, their other plays should show some of the more inventive traits that we have found in the implied staging of *Sir Thomas More*. The argument is not that collaborating hacks can do good work once but that they do it typically. We have found an ironic mode of staging in *More*, with different fictional locations being drawn into one stage area as a visual notation of their relation to one another. Does such a visual design appear in other plays written by the likes of Hand A and Hand B?

With this question in mind, I have read the other plays written for the Admiral's men at the time we suppose *Sir Thomas More* was being revised for them (the same plays I compared to *More* in terms of casting characteristics), and although each of these deserves an essay to itself, it will be appropriate here to take note of the two most obvious examples of the kind of ironic visual dramaturgy we have been discussing.[7]

When You See Me You Know Me, the Admiral's play that most resembles *Sir Thomas More* in casting implications, structure, and subject matter, employs a divided-stage technique common in Elizabethan plays, by which one part of the stage is a focal area (often a shop) and the rest is a broad expanse (often a street running in front of the shop). This technique does not depend on special staging devices like the pavilion or booth we have imagined for *More,* but when a pavilion was used it would serve for the focal area. In the first and third sections of *When You See Me,* the stage is divided between a broad expanse that stands for the presence chamber (see ll. 630, 1862, 1948, 1983, 2220, and 2467 of the Malone Society edition), while the adjacent focal area is the furnished private room of the King. When the King first appears in his private room, the direction reads "Enter king within" (l. 576), which suggests that some sort of structural device separates his room from the presence chamber. Later in the

7. Alan C. Dessen's concept of "linking analogues" is similar to the visual repetition I have in mind. See his *Elizabethan Drama and the Viewer's Eye* (Chapel Hill: Univ. of North Carolina Press, 1977), passim, and *Elizabethan Stage Conventions and Modern Interpreters* (Cambridge: Cambridge Univ. Press, 1984), passim. Madeleine Doran's *Endeavors of Art* (Madison: Univ. of Wisconsin Press, 1954) describes Elizabethan multiple plots in terms that can be related to staging, as Dessen shows. See also Richard Levin, *The Multiple Plot in English Renaissance Drama* (Chicago: Univ. of Chicago Press, 1971); Mark Rose, *Shakespearean Design* (Cambridge: Harvard Univ. Press, 1972); David Bevington, *Action Is Eloquence: Shakespeare's Language of Gesture* (Cambridge: Harvard Univ. Press, 1984); and Norman Rabkin, *Shakespeare and the Common Understanding* (New York: Free Press, 1967), for further explorations of the artistic temperament that lies behind this stagecraft. For studies of *More* which respect the aesthetic design of the play, see Judith Doolin Spikes, "*The Book of Sir Thomas More:* Structure and Meaning," *Moreana,* 11 (1974), 25–39; Charles R. Forker and Joseph Candido, "Wit, Wisdom, and Theatricality in *The Book of Sir Thomas More,*" *Shakespeare Studies,* 13 (1980), 85–104; G. Harold Metz, "the Master of the Revels and *The Booke of Sir Thomas Moore,*" *Shakespeare Quarterly,* 33 (1982), 493–495.

same scene (ll. 711 ff.), Will Sommers plays a prank on the King by remaining on the broad expanse of the platform and directing the business occurring in the private room. This is the same combination of stage areas found in *Sir Thomas More,* with the explicit indication of a special stage structure being provided in this case by the word "within" at line 576 (there is no explicit mention of curtains in this play).

The ironic staging occurs in the middle section of the play, when the King's private room is a prison cell. That is, when the King practices his "gests" and goes to prison, he actually goes to the same space that serves as his private room at court. The stage direction "Enter the King in Prison" (l. 1231) implies that the "within" structure from the court scenes is being used, but the point is made into an explicit joke when the King says:

> Well M. Constable, you have made the Counter
> This night, the royall Court of Englands King.
> [ll. 1251–1252]

The same joke—that the prison is the court, the court the prison—continues throughout this part of the play (see l. 1326 and l. 1397). Obviously one stage structure serves for ironically different locations.

The same thing can be seen in the second of our brief examples, *1 Honest Whore.* In three scenes, Candido's shop stands juxtaposed to part of the open platform, which signifies a street (see I, v; III, i; and IV, iii, in Bowers's edition of Dekker). In the shop are displayed the fine lawns and cambrics of what is here taken to be honest commerce. Bellafront's room, by contrast, contains the cosmetics and ornaments of the whorish trade (see II, i and III, iii). The one scene set in Hippolito's room (IV, i) carries the idea a stage further by displaying the meditative properties of skull, book, and picture. The visual dramaturgy is the same as in *Sir Thomas More,* with stage properties (like the furniture in *More*) serving as emblems of contrasts in social standing. Of course different stage areas could be used for these different interiors, but the *final* interior space of *1 Honest Whore* makes it clear that the other spaces have been located here too, as they are in *Sir Thomas More*. The final interior space is literally an enclosure. It is a cage for the madmen in Bedlam, and it has to be opened to view. One of the madmen is a parody of Hippolito, another is a parody of Candido. Where else in the play would this enclosure be used? The space of the madmen's parody, it seems obvious, is the space of the objects of their parody—Candido's shop and Hippolito's room. How Bellafront's room figures in the Bedlam scene requires more than the quick survey appropriate here, but the point of the play's visual design can be seen. The merchant's shop, the whore's dressing room, the ascetic's room—if they are all the same place in the end, they are the cage of madmen. This is not a sunny play.

That is a glimpse of what could, treated fully, become a major topic: the visual design of plays for the Admiral's men. Each Elizabethan company could be studied from that perspective. I see no reason to doubt that all the companies practiced visual design in the theatre or that they competed with one another in developing their own styles. "Style" and "design" are modern words for the practice of visually significant stagecraft, but that practice is about as old as the theatre itself. For the moment, however, our concern must be with the manuscript at hand, for there is an important piece of unfinished business to consider for the writers of *Sir Thomas More*.

If it appears that these writers designed the major interiors of the play for one enclosurelike space, it must also appear that they were painting themselves into a corner. Two of the original interiors which we would read into one space happen to follow immediately after one another: The Lord Mayor's scene at More's house leads directly to the council-chamber scene in which More refuses to sign the King's articles. How could two successive scenes have been staged in the same space if they require different furnishings? There appears to be no time to replace the seats over which More makes his little fuss with the formal furniture of the council table and chairs, over which he also makes a little fuss. This implied staging runs into a problem that the American musical used to solve by adding episodes and songs to be staged in front of the curtain while the set was being changed—the problem of the "clash." The Elizabethans were not changing sets, of course, but they did need some time to replace the Chelsea furniture with the council furniture, the difference between the two being fundamental markers in the stages of More's career.

Moreover, in turning to the revision of the play—for the visual design I have been describing belongs to the original text—we find that a second clash has been created by those very playwrights who seemed to be careful about such practical aspects of the theatre as casting and doubling. The revisers combined the Erasmus episode with a scene staged separately in the original, More's encounter with the long-haired ruffian Faulkner. The original Faulkner scene took place in an exterior, Paternoster Row, but the revision brings Faulkner to More's study just as More is preparing to welcome Erasmus. The result of this decision is another clash, for the new Erasmus-Faulkner scene is followed by the welcoming of the Lord Mayor at More's house. Since the welcoming scene leads into the council-chamber scene, we have in the revised text three interiors in a row, and thus two clashes according to our hypothesis about the repeated use of a curtained space. Could playwrights so shrewd as to solve a practical casting problem with the combined Erasmus-Faulkner scene and so inventive as to create a visual design for their play be so stupid as to make the entire business impractical by running three curtained interiors together?

The answer to this question reveals one more way in which specific theatrical purposes lie behind the patches of revision in the manuscript. The first two of the three consecutive interiors are constructed according to the common divided-stage technique we discussed earlier. Whether the division is imaginary or physical, this kind of scene always has one area as a central focus and the other area as a broad expanse. In the combined Erasmus-Faulkner scene in *Sir Thomas More*, the focal area is More's study, furnished with table and chairs. Erasmus approaches from a distance (Addition IV, ll. 92–122)—that is, he crosses the broad expanse and enters the focal area of the study. (Again, this separation of spaces occurs whether or not a physical enclosure defines the focal area.) Moreover, the long-haired Faulkner's appearances in this scene would have to be played a little apart from the study, on the broad expanse, so that More can be shown in the comic situation of shuttling between a tawdry ruffian just outside the study and Europe's greatest man of learning just inside.

The entertainment of the Lord Mayor fits the same pattern of spacing. It is a play-within-the-play, a type of scene which focuses on the spectators (on the leading spectator, to be specific, who is usually a king or a duke) and uses the broad expanse as the playing area for the actors. The seats for the Lord Mayor and his entourage define the focal area, and the broad expanse of the platform is available for the interlude performed by the visiting players. In both scenes, the area of the central focus is used in conjunction with the broader expanse of the platform to give an impression of slight separation between two spaces.

The point to grasp about both scenes is that they conclude out on the broad expanse. By the end of the first of these scenes, More and Erasmus have exited, and Faulkner and his master remain behind to conclude the scene. They would not remain in More's study. They would remain on the broad expanse of the platform, where Faulkner would always stand. Indeed, this is the very part of the scene which we can see being progressively lengthened by Hands C and E in the revision: C thought to have Faulkner and his master exit at line 204, with a messenger entering to begin the next scene. He then crossed out the messenger's entrance, copied about ten more lines for Faulkner and his master, wrote "exit" for them, changed his mind and gave way to Hand E, who added thirty lines more between Faulkner and his master. It is perfectly clear that these writers are padding the scene's conclusion so as to add time for something, and if my earlier assumption that they were adding time for the sake of casting does not stand by itself, I offer the present assumption that they were adding time for the furniture to be changed in the curtained space that stood for More's study, the real point being that shrewd theatre people know to do both things at once.

The second clash reveals exactly the same pattern. After the play-within-the-play, the Lord Mayor's entourage leaves the area of central focus, while the players remain behind where they have acted. The original version gives the players only eleven lines before the council-chamber scene begins. In the revision Hand B adds some sixty-five lines for the players, providing ample time for rearranging the curtained space for the council-chamber scene.

In short, the problem of clashes seems to have been anticipated by the writers. There was a doorway in that corner they were painting themselves into. The original play had a visual design that depended on the curtained space explicitly mentioned in scene ii. The revisers, by combining the Erasmus-Faulkner scenes, for reasons of casting, I suppose, but also perhaps for reasons of aesthetics, created a new clash and then eliminated it by padding the end of the scene in a move which also provided more time for costume changes. That is how the theatre does its work—by creating problems for itself and then solving them. The revisers also padded the ending of the next interior scene in order to improve casting, or lengthen the time available for setting the council chamber, or both. That all this patching and filling was done in the interests of an artistic design need surprise no one who has worked on an artistic design. They all require patching and filling. Perhaps the occasional play was handed to an Elizabethan company with all the practical problems solved from the beginning, a sort of promptbook *ab ovo*. Such a text does not sound like the theatre to me. It sounds like the legend from which the genius-author springs to life, the canonizing legend.

I think the manuscript of *Sir Thomas More* is better finished than is commonly thought, better designed, better revised, but most to the point, better representative of the theatres in which it was put together. If one of those theatres was the Fortune, where the Admiral's men had it revised to join such plays, also visually designed, as *When You See Me* and *1 Honest Whore*, I should like to turn now to the other theatre, the Rose, for which the original version seems to have been intended. We have abundant evidence about staging at the Rose—so abundant that the subject deserves a chapter to itself—and I would like to explore further the possibility that the particular structure for raised and interior scenes that we have inferred in *Sir Thomas More* was in fact employed in the repertory performed there.

6

Staging at the Rose

My purpose in this chapter is to undertake an excursion that will bring two phases of the argument advanced in earlier chapters into contact with each other. As I describe the visual design of *Sir Thomas More* in the previous chapter, readers may well wonder if the implied staging of this one play is congruent with the separate hypothesis that *Sir Thomas More* was originally written for Strange's men at the Rose playhouse in the earlier 1590s. If Strange's men can be said from their acknowledged plays never to have used the curtained and raised areas implied by *Sir Thomas More*, for example, then perhaps I have misread *Sir Thomas More* or misassigned it to Strange's men at the Rose.

We must remain clear about what is entailed in pursuing such questions. Bringing hypotheses together is a procedure of skepticism. It cannot prove any of the hypotheses, but it can put them to a test that may invalidate one or both of them. This is the kind of test I earlier applied to evidence about casting, when I placed the implied casting of the revised *Sir Thomas More* next to the implied casting of other plays of the Admiral's men to see if the patterns were similar. In finding similar patterns, I did not prove that *More* was revised for the Admiral's men; I showed, instead, that a skeptic's eye for the negative result was not to be satisfied here. The more often that can be done, the stronger become the odds that the present hypothesis will stand up. But better odds do not prove anything.

Piety in behalf of skepticism is not the only purpose of this excursion. In remarking that theatre historians had succeeded in describing most Elizabethan theatres by close and patient study of evidence, I withheld the opinion that one playhouse, the Rose, has not been well examined. The book devoted to the subject, Ernest L. Rhodes's *Henslowe's Rose: The Stage and Staging,* is bent on demonstrating a Vitruvian design which, in my opinion, must be forcibly read into the internal evidence of the play texts.[1] This is not the place for a fullfledged study of the Rose or a debate with Rhodes's method, but a fresh preliminary view of the evidence will show the outlines of work remaining to be done on this important playhouse. In addition to testing two hypotheses about *Sir Thomas More* against each other, then, I wish to make a beginning—nothing more—on a new survey of staging at the Rose.

What brings these two purposes together is the question of special staging areas. If *Sir Thomas More* is designed around such special areas as a curtained enclosure and a raised space, the obvious question is what do texts known to have been performed at the Rose show about these two kinds of special staging? Contained in this question is the further possibility implied in *Sir Thomas More,* that the curtained area and the raised area were parts of one stage structure, a projecting pavilion, but there is no reason to assume such a combination in a preliminary survey of the evidence. We are simply asking of the Rose plays: to what extent do they show a curtained exclosure? to what extent a raised acting area? How these special staging spaces relate to

1. Ernest L. Rhodes, *Henslowe's Rose: The Stage and Staging* (Lexington: Univ. of Kentucky Press, 1976).

each other will become an answerable question before we finish, I believe, but it must be deferred for the moment.

More than three dozen published or manuscript plays can, with greater confidence than is usual in affairs of this sort, be assigned to the Rose. The confidence comes from Henslowe's *Diary*, which is unique in providing daily repertory lists as well as accounting records for new plays as they were readied for production. Thus extant play texts can be connected to the titles in Henslowe's *Diary* to give us a reliable body of evidence for the Rose. Some of these texts are more reliable than others, and in a complete study discriminations would have to be made. For our purposes here, however, the plays can be surveyed as a single group to see what unmistakable evidence they offer about special staging areas. I wish to emphasize "unmistakable." We are looking for explicit stage directions that spell out the staging (the kind of direction that indicates the curtained enclosure for scene ii of *Sir Thomas More*, for example), or implicit staging that is so clear as to be self-evident. I have said that the reader of an Elizabethan play must have a theatrical imagination in order to see the implied staging that lies behind the laconic stage directions, but imaginative readings of the Rose plays are not the order of business for now. I do not want to bury what I hope is an imaginative reading of *Sir Thomas More* under three dozen others. This is a survey of evidence which I believe anyone can see.

Here is a list of the plays I connect to the Rose.[2] The basis for

2. My list agrees for the most part with that of Rhodes, *Henslowe's Rose*, pp. 185–223, but our differences can be summarized. I exclude the following titles included by Rhodes on grounds that the identifications between published title and Henslowe's title are too speculative to be convincing: *Captain Thomas Stukley* (Henslowe's "Stewtley"), *Golden Age* (Henslowe's "Seleo and Olympo"), *Silver Age* (Henslowe's "1 Hercules"), *Bronze Age* (Henslowe's "2 Hercules"), *Famous Victories of Henry V* (Henslowe's "Henry V"), *John a Kent* (Henslowe's "Wiseman of WestChester"), *Four Prentices of London* (Henslowe's "Godfrey of Bulloigne"), *Jupiter and Io* (Henslowe's "Five Plays in One"). I have included the following texts (excluded by Rhodes) for reasons given in the list below under each title: *2 Seven Deadly Sins*, *Blind Beggar of Bednall Green*, *Sir Thomas Wyatt*, *1 Tamar Cam*, and *John of Bordeaux*.

the selections lies for the most part in W. W. Greg, ed., *Henslowe's Diary*, 2 vols. (London: Bullen, 1904); Greg, ed., *Dramatic Documents from the Elizabethan Playhouses*, 2 vols. (Oxford: Clarendon Press, 1931); E. K. Chambers, *The Elizabethan Stage*, 4 vols. (Oxford: Clarendon Presss, 1923). I have also benefited from the advice of Professors S. P. Cerasano and Roslyn Knutson on these matters.

1. *Alphonsus of Aragon.* Q 1599.
   Because of a reference to "old Mahomet's head" in Henslowe's inventory (such a property is needed in *Alphonsus*), this piece may appear in the Rose repertory under the title of "Mahomet."
   Text: Malone Society Reprint, ed. W. W. Greg (Oxford, 1926).

2. *Battle of Alcazar.* Manuscript plot.
   The plot surely falls between 1594 and 1602 and was prepared either for the Rose or the Fortune. Greg and Chambers played out a long argument over the date, Greg insisting on 1598–1599 (Rose) and Chambers upholding the possibility of 1600–1602 (Fortune).[3]
   Text: Greg, ed., *Dramatic Documents*, II.

3. *Battle of Alcazar.* Q 1594.
   This text, printed without entry in 1594, with the Admiral's men specified on the title page, may be Henslowe's "Muly Molocco" or his "Mahomet."
   Text: Malone Society Reprint, ed. W. W. Greg (Oxford, 1907).

4. *The Blind Beggar of Alexandria.* Q 1598.
   A new play for the Admiral's men at the Rose on 12 February 1596 and part of their repertory until 1 April 1597. Published in 1598 (Stationers' Register 15 August 1598), as acted by the Admiral's men.

---

3. To follow the argument in order: Greg, *Two Elizabethan Stage Abridgements* (Oxford: Malone Society, 1923), pp. 85–93; Chambers, *Elizabethan Stage*, II, 175–177; Greg, *Dramatic Documents*, I, 24–42. In a note in the last source, Chambers capitulated before the persistent energy of Greg, but the evidence remains ambiguous. Greg's theory depends on Alleyn's return to the stage in 1598–1599, a hypothesis that wants support.

STAGING AT THE ROSE

Text: Malone Society Reprint, ed. W. W. Greg (Oxford, 1928).

5. *Blind Beggar of Bednall Green.* Q 1659.
Played by the Admiral's men in 1600, just before their move to the Fortune.
Text: Tudor Facsimile Texts, ed. J. S. Farmer, 1914.

6. *David and Bethsabe.* Q 1599.
Although Greg (*Diary*, II, 232) and Chambers (*Elizabethan Stage*, III, 461) remained unconvinced of the possibility, I follow Rhodes (p. 222) in connecting this text with Henslowe's reference to "poles and workmanship for to hang Absalom." In the text, Absalom is required to hang by the hair for over 100 lines.
Text: *David and Bethsabe*, ed. Elmer Blistein, in *The Dramatic Works of George Peele*, gen. ed. C. T. Prouty, Vol. 3 (New Haven: Yale Univ. Press, 1970).

7. *Doctor Faustus.* Q 1604.
An old play when Henslowe first recorded it in 1594. In all there are records of twenty-five performances at the Rose.
Text: *Marlowe's Doctor Faustus: 1604–1616*, ed. W. W. Greg (Oxford, 1950).

8. *Doctor Faustus.* Q 1616.
Another version, with different staging implications. It is best to treat these as separate plays for our purposes.
Text: see *Faustus* Q 1604.

9. *Downfall of the Earl of Huntington.* Q 1601;
Death of the Earl of Huntington. Q 1601.
Henslowe paid Munday for *The Downfall* on 15 February 1598 and Munday and Chettle for *The Death* between 20 February and 8 March in the same year. Both parts were licensed at the end of March, and they must have been ready for production about that time. The two parts were entered in S.R. on 1 December 1600, and both were published in 1601, as acted by the Admiral's men. The plays were obviously designed together and are treated as a single unit here.
Text: Malone Society Reprint, ed. John C. Meagher: *Downfall* (Oxford, 1964); *Death* (Oxford, 1965).

10. *Edward I.* Q 1593.
    Although Chambers was skeptical of this possibility (*Elizabethan Stage*, III, 460), Frank S. Hook argues persuasively for identifying the published play with the "Longshanks" listed by Henslowe for 1595–1596. See *The Dramatic Works of George Peele*, gen. ed. C. T. Prouty, Vol. 2 (New Haven: Yale Univ. Press, 1961), p. 7.
    Text: see *Dramatic Works of Peele*, above.

11. *Fortune's Tennis.* Manuscript plot.
    Greg (*Dramatic Documents*, I, 131) shows that this fragment of a plot comes from the Admiral's men, but a question remains about its date. Possibly, as Greg argues, it was prepared about 1597–1598 at the Rose, although no title in Henslowe's *Diary* before 1600 clearly corresponds to the plot. Moreover, in September 1600, when the Admiral's men were ready to move to the Fortune, Henslowe records "fortewn tenes," perhaps in connection with a version of the play for the new theatre. The evidence remains evenly balanced between the Rose and the Fortune.
    Text: Greg, ed., *Dramatic Documents*, II.

12. *Frederick and Basilea.* Manuscript plot.
    A new play for the Admiral's men on 3 June 1597. It was probably not published, but Greg (*Dramatic Documents*, I, 123) presents clear evidence that the extant manuscript plot was drawn up for the Admiral's men in June or July of 1597, during the play's run at the Rose.
    Text: Greg, ed., *Dramatic Documents*, II.

13. *Friar Bacon and Friar Bungay.* Q 1594.
    The Queen's men are named on the title page, and Henslowe names that company for a Rose production in 1594. (The "Friar Bacon" played by Strange's men in 1592 was probably *John of Bordeaux*, q.v.)
    Text: Malone Society Reprint, ed. W. W. Greg (Oxford, 1926).

14. *George a Green, the Pinner of Wakefield.* Q 1599.
    Sussex's men, who are named on the title page, performed it at the Rose in 1593–1594.
    Text: Malone Society Reprint, ed. P. W. Clarke and W. W. Greg (Oxford, 1911).

15. *1 Henry VI.* Shakespeare Folio, 1623.
Recorded, apparently as a new play, for Strange's men at the
Rose on 3 March 1592, but not published before the 1623
Folio.
Text: *The First Folio of Shakespeare*, facsimile edition, ed.
Charlton Hinman (New York: Norton, 1968).

16. *Humorous Day's Mirth (Comedy of Humours).* Q 1599.
Henslowe records a *Comedy of Humours* as a new play on 11
May 1597. It continued in the repertory of the Admiral's
men throughout that year. The identification of this piece
with Chapman's *Humorous Day's Mirth* is made virtually certain by the listing in Henslowe's 1598 inventory of Verone's
son's hose and Labesha's cloak. Chapman's play was printed
without S.R. entry in 1599, as acted by the Admiral's men.
Text: Malone Society Reprint, ed. W. W. Greg and D. Nichol
Smith (Oxford, 1938).

17. *The Jew of Malta.* Q 1633.
Each company at the Rose before 1600 performed *The Jew of
Malta.* The title was entered in S.R. in 1594, but the extant
edition was not published until 1633. Henslowe's 1598 inventory lists a cauldron "for the Jew." This is used in the final
scene.
Text: *Complete Works of Marlowe*, ed. Fredson Bowers (Cambridge: Cambridge Univ. Press, 1973), Vol. 1.

18. *John of Bordeaux.* Manuscript play.
This manuscript play on the Friar Bacon legend names an
actor from Strange's men of the early 1590s and is probably
the piece Henslowe lists for that company as *Friar Bacon* in
1592–1593. Greene's better-known *Friar Bacon and Friar
Bungay* was played at the Rose by a different company, the
Queen's men. See Scott McMillin, "The Ownership of *The
Jew of Malta, Friar Bacon*, and *The Ranger's Comedy*," *English
Language Notes*, 9 (1972), 249–252.
Text: Malone Society Reprint, ed. W. L. Renwick (Oxford,
1936).

19. *King Leire.* Q 1605.
Played by Sussex's and Queen's men at the Rose in April
1594. A month later (14 May) the title was entered in S.R.,
but no corresponding edition is extant. In 1605 a new S.R.
entry was soon followed by the only extant version.

Text: Malone Society Reprint, ed. W. W. Greg and R. Warwick Bond (Oxford, 1907).

20. *A Knack to Know an Honest Man.* Q 1596.

An important play in the Admiral's repertory from the time Henslowe entered it on 22 October 1594 until its last recorded performance at the Rose on 3 November 1596, the year of publication (S.R., 26 November 1595). No company is named on the title page, but the close connection between the play's printing and its appearances in the Admiral's repertory eliminates doubt that the text comes from the Rose.

Text: Malone Society Reprint, ed. H. de Vocht and W. W. Greg (Oxford, 1910).

21. *A Knack to Know a Knave.* Q 1594.

Henslowe lists this title for Strange's men on 10 June 1592, and it continued at the Rose until 24 January 1593. On 7 January 1594 it was entered in S.R., and the text was published in the same year. Both the S.R. entry and the quarto title page name Alleyn's company, and refer to "Kemps applauded Merrimentes of the men of Goteham. . . ." The references are clearly to Strange's men.

Text: Malone Society Reprint, ed. G. R. Proudfoot (Oxford, 1963).

22. *Look about You.* Q 1600.

The Admiral's men are named on the title page of the 1600 quarto. The play must belong to the series of King John and Robin Hood plays which Robert Wilson, Chettle, Munday, and others were writing for the Admiral's men in the late 1590s. Henslowe does not use this title, but there is a gap in the theatrical entries of late April–early May 1599, when the other King John and Robin Hood plays were current.

Text: Malone Society Reprint, ed. W. W. Greg (Oxford, 1913).

23. *Looking Glass for London and England.* Q 1594.

Henslowe lists "the lockinglasse" for Strange's men in 1592, although no company is named on the title page.

Text: Malone Society Reprint, ed. W. W. Greg (Oxford, 1932).

24. *Massacre at Paris.* Q n.d., circa 1594.

Henslowe marked "the tragedy of the guyes" new in January

of 1593, and under that title or "the masacer," the play had a vigorous history among Henslowe's companies: Strange's men originated it in 1593, the Admiral's men revived it in 1594, probably in 1598, and certainly in 1602 (at the Fortune). The extant octavo, which appeared without S.R. entry carries no date on the title page. Greg's survey of the evidence (introduction to Malone Society Reprint, pp. vii–viii) suggests 1594. The Admiral's men, who revived the play in 1594, are named on the title page.

Text: *Complete Works of Marlowe,* ed. Fredson Bowers (Cambridge: Cambridge Univ. Press, 1973), Vol. 1.

25. *Old Fortunatus.* Q 1600.
From February to May 1596 the Admiral's men revived a first part of "Fortunatus." Presumably they had a second part in their repertory, although Henslowe mentions none by name, for in 1599 Dekker was paid for "the hole hystory of Fortunatus." The newly fashioned play, now complete in one part, was prepared for court early in December, Dekker receiving payments for altering the book and for rewriting the ending. The court performance fell on 27 December 1599, and the play was printed in 1600, "as it was plaied before the Queenes Maiestie this Christmas."

Text: *Dramatic Works of Thomas Dekker,* ed. Fredson Bowers, Vol. 1 (Cambridge: Cambridge Univ. Press, 1953).

26. *Orlando Furioso.* Q 1594.
Recorded only once at the Rose, for Strange's men on 21 February 1592. S.R. entry in 1593 and again in 1594, published in 1594, as played before the Queen. The extant manuscript "part" does not add to the broad questions of staging being considered here.

Text: Malone Society Reprint, ed. W. W. Greg and R. B. McKerrow (Oxford, 1907).

27. *Patient Grissell.* Q 1603.
Henslowe paid Chettle, Dekker, and William Haughton "in earnest" of this play during the last three months of 1599. Production must have occurred early after the turn of the year, for in January Henslowe bought a grey gown for Grissell. Soon some sort of trouble arose about publication: Henslowe, on 18 March 1600, moved "to staye the printing"; ten days later the play was entered in S.R. for C. Burby; the

quarto, which did not appear until 1603, was printed for Henry Rocket (who had been Burby's apprentice until 31 January 1602). The Admiral's men are named on the title page. It would seem that Henslowe prevented a surreptitious edition soon after the play was produced in 1600, and made some arrangement with Burby to publish a good text after the play's first commercial attraction had lessened.

Text: *Dramatic Works of Thomas Dekker,* ed. Fredson Bowers, Vol. 1 (Cambridge: Cambridge Univ. Press, 1953).

28. *2 Seven Deadly Sins.* Manuscript plot
The plot names actors otherwise known to have been with Strange's men in the early 1590s. Greg dates the production before the beginning of Henslowe's daily lists, but it has been thought to carry over to the lists as "iiii playes in one," recorded at the Rose for 6 March 1592.

Text: Greg, ed., *Dramatic Documents,* II.

29. *The Shoemakers' Holiday (The Gentle Craft).* Q 1600.
Henslowe paid Dekker for this play in 1599. The Quarto of 1600 names the Admiral's men on the title page.

Text: *Dramatic Works of Thomas Dekker,* ed. Fredson Bowers, Vol. 1 (Cambridge: Cambridge Univ. Press, 1953).

30. *1 Sir John Oldcastle.* Q 1600.
The *Diary* shows that Munday, Drayton, Wilson, and Richard Hathway were at work on a two-part play about Oldcastle in October 1599. Early in November Henslowe paid 10 s. to the poets "at the playing of *Sir John Oldscastle* the first time." The entry must pertain to Part I, for Dekker was still being paid for the second part in December. Both parts were entered in S.R. on 11 August 1600, and Part I was published in the same year, as acted by the Admiral's men. No edition of Part II remains.

Text: Malone Society Reprint, ed. Percy Simpson and W. W. Greg (Oxford, 1908).

31. *Sir Thomas Wyatt.* Q 1607.
Chambers and Greg identify the extant *Sir Thomas Wyatt* with a play, or perhaps a two-part play, which Henslowe called "Lady Jane" (*Henslowe's Diary,* II, 232; *Elizabethan Stage,* III, 293–294). If the identification is right, the play was written in 1602 by Dekker and Webster, among others, for Worcester's men at the Rose. Worcester's men later became Queen

STAGING AT THE ROSE

Anne's men, and the latter company is named on the title page of *Wyatt*, which appeared without S.R. entry in 1607.

Text: *Dramatic Works of Thomas Dekker*, ed. Fredson Bowers, Vol. 1 (Cambridge: Cambridge Univ. Press, 1953).

32. *The Spanish Tragedy*. Q n.d., circa 1592.
Henslowe lists "Jeronymo" for Strange's men in 1592. The play was entered in the S.R. on 6 October that year. The undated Q probably appeared in 1592–1593. The enlarged Q of 1602 is not considered here, for it may have been prepared for a revival at the Fortune in 1601–1602.

Text: Malone Society Reprint, ed. W. W. Greg and D. Nichol Smith (Oxford, 1948).

33. *1 Tamar Cam*. Manuscript plot.
Henslowe recorded Part I for the Rose in June 1596. This was probably a revision, for Part II had been performed at the Rose in 1592, and one would suppose that Part I also existed by then. Greg (*Dramatic Documents*, I, 160–161) suggests that the plot was prepared as late as 1602, for the Admiral's men at the Fortune.

Text: Greg, ed., *Dramatic Documents*, II.

34. *1 and 2 Tamburlaine*. Q 1590.
Both parts were published in 1590, as played by the Admiral's men. Henslowe records Part I in August 1594 for the Admiral's men and the play was a popular piece in repertory until November 1595, when entries for it cease abruptly. All entries for Part II fall within the same period. The sequel was played about half as often as Part I, and usually in tandem with it. The plays were obviously designed for the same staging system, so I treat them as a single unit.

Text: *Complete Works of Marlowe*, ed. Fredson Bowers (Cambridge: Cambridge Univ. Press, 1973), Vol. 1.

35. *Titus Andronicus*. Q 1594.
The *Diary* shows that Sussex's men played *Titus Andronicus* as a new piece in January and February of 1594. Their season was abruptly brought to a close, probably by the plague, and their last performance—the play was *Titus Andronicus*—fell on 6 February. On the same day *Titus Andronicus* was entered in the S.R. by John Danter, who published it before the end of the year, naming Sussex's men with other companies on the title page.

Text: *Titus Andronicus: The First Quarto* (in facsimile), ed., Joseph Quincy Adams (New York: Scribner's, 1936).

36. *Troilus and Cressida.* Manuscript plot.

Only a fragment remains of this plot, but it includes enough evidence to allow Greg (*Dramatic Documents*, I, 138) to identify the company as the Admiral's men between March 1598 and July 1600. In April 1599 Dekker and Chettle were working on a *Troilus and Cressida* for the Admiral's men, and it was probably for the original performance of their play that the plot was prepared.

Text: Greg, ed., *Dramatic Documents*, II.

37. *Two Angry Women of Abington.* Q 1599.

From December 1598 to February 1599, Henry Porter was paid for what seems to be a second part of this play. The published text, which appeared without S.R. entry in 1599, as played by the Admiral's men, offers no indication of whether it is the first or second part. Quite possibly it presents both parts together. The text runs over 3,000 lines, tells a complete story, and gives no hint either of a predecessor or of a sequel. Both Greg (*Diary*, II, 193) and Chambers (*Elizabethan Stage*, III, 467) think that the text gives us only Part I, which they associate with Porter's "Love Prevented," written for Henslowe in 1598. A pun on the theatre's name seems likely in the concluding address to the audience ("Rosasolis" at line 3028).

Text: Malone Society Reprint, ed. W. W. Greg (Oxford, 1912).

38. *Woman Killed with Kindness.* Q 1607.

Henslowe paid Heywood for this play early in 1603, on behalf of Worcester's men at the Rose. The play was published without S.R. entry in 1607.

Text: *Woman Killed with Kindness*, ed. R. W. Van Fossen (Cambridge: Harvard Univ. Press, 1961). Revels Edition.

39. *Woman Will Have Her Will*, or *Englishmen for My Money.* Q 1616.

Henslowe paid Haughton for *Woman Will Have Her Will* in 1598. William White entered the title in S.R. in 1601 and published it in 1616.

Text: Malone Society Reprint, ed. W. W. Greg (Oxford, 1912).

Of this abundant evidence we ask direct, simple questions. Do
the texts contain explicit references to raised or enclosure staging? If so, how often? Taking explicit indications of raised staging first, we find that nearly half of the Rose plays (18, or 46
percent) remain silent about this possibility:

Alphonsus of Aragon	*Knack to Know an Honest Man*
Battle of Alcazar, quarto	*Knack to Know a Knave*
Blind Beggar of Bednall Green	*Old Fortunatus*
Doctor Faustus, Q 1604	*Patient Grissell*
Fortune's Tennis, fragmentary plot	2 *Seven Deadly Sins*
Friar Bacon and Friar Bungay	*Shoemakers' Holiday*
Humorous Day's Mirth	*Sir John Oldcastle*
John of Bordeaux	1 *Tamar Cam*
King Leire	*Woman Killed with Kindness*

Another eight texts (21 percent) require raised action once
apiece. These eight scenes show an important consistency: in
each, no more than two characters appear above, with the possible exception of the unnumbered musicians in *Look about You,*
and their appearances are usually quite brief. Here are the examples, with line and page numbers referring to the texts cited
in the alphabetical list of Rose plays:

> *Blind Beggar of Alexandria,* l. 354. One character "above on
> the walls" for soliloquy of 15 lines.
> *Doctor Faustus,* Q 1616, p. 241. One character "above at a
> window," speaking to others below for 160 lines.
> *Frederick and Basilea.* Two characters "upon the walls"
> speak to others, then "come down."
> *George a Green,* l. 299. One character "on the walls" speaks
> to others below for 60 lines.
> *Look about You,* l. 2170. Musicians are said to be at "this
> window" for length of song.
> *Orlando Furioso,* l. 394. One character "upon the walls"
> speaks to another below for 45 lines.
> *Sir Thomas Wyatt,* p. 441. One character enters "upon the
> walls" and speaks to others below for 30 lines.
> *Two Angry Women of Abington,* l. 1495. One character "in the
> window" speaks to others below for 90 lines.

Thus two-thirds of the Rose plays either make no reference to raised action or call for only one small scene "above." These texts imply no raised staging area beyond what can be seen in the Swan drawing, our one approach to eye-witness evidence about the public theatres. The Swan drawing shows a gallery running above and behind the platform stage. The gallery seems to be a place for spectators or musicians, but one of its compartments could easily have been used for such small "window" and "wall" scenes as we have noticed before. The one or two characters in the raised position usually speak to others on the platform below. No depth is required for the raised area, in other words. Characters there are held in relation to others on the platform, and nothing more than the narrow gallery shown in the Swan drawing is indicated.

The results are different for the remaining plays, each of which makes two or more explicit calls for raised action. The intriguing thing about this group is that it includes all examples of extensive raised scenes, scenes which involve large groups of characters "above" and which run to considerable length or require stage depth for the blocking: the assembly of senators in *Titus Andronicus,* for example, where the raised area is used in conjunction with the platform for the entire first act, or the royal audience for Hieronimo's climactic play-within-the-play in *The Spanish Tragedy,* or the siege of Orleans in *1 Henry VI.* Here is a list of all the raised episodes in this group, with the extensive scenes so labeled.

> *Battle of Alcazar,* plot, l. 25. Four characters stage a dumb-show "above."
>
> l. 56. At least four characters (the plot is decayed here) stage a dumb-show "above."
>
> *David and Bethsabe,* p. 193. "David sits above viewing" Bethsabe, who is discovered within a curtained enclosure. Eventually three characters are on the raised space, interacting among themselves. Raised area used for 150 lines.
>
> p. 198. Extensive. Two characters with attendants, "upon the walls," which are then assaulted and taken by opposing

forces from the platform. Three victors remain "above" and speak among themselves. Raised area used for 60 lines and much business.

Death of Huntington, l. 1570. "Enter, or above," two characters who speak to others below for 15 lines.

l. 2123. "Enter, on the wall," two characters who speak to others below for 90 lines.

l. 2702. Extensive. One character remains "on the walls" for over 300 lines and opens a gate or window he has rigged, revealing the corpses of his mother and brother to others below.

Edward I, p. 100. At least five characters enter "on the walls" and speak to others below (with some interaction among themselves—one is being tortured by the rest) for 175 lines.

p. 147. One character makes "the proclamation upon the walls." Length cannot be determined—there is no text of the proclamation.

1 Henry VI, I, iv. Extensive. Four characters speak among themselves "on the turrets" before two are gunned down, occasioning a threnody from one of the survivors. 90 lines.

I, vi. Four characters speak among themselves "on the walls," accompanied by soldiers. 30 lines.

II, i. Extensive. Three characters with soldiers scale the walls and force the French to "leap o'er the walls in their shirts." Few lines, but much business.

III, ii. One character "on the top, thrusting out a torch burning." 3 lines.

IV, ii. One character with soldiers "aloft," speaking to others below for 40 lines.

V, iii. One character "on the walls" speaks to others below for 20 lines.

Jew of Malta, p. 298. One character appears "above" and observes others below for 5 lines.

p. 331. Extensive. One character enters "with a hammer above, very busy," and puts the finishing touches on a two-level staging device. This becomes the scene of its maker's downfall when he falls through a trap in the raised area and is discovered in a boiling cauldron below. Raised action for 65 lines.

Looking Glass for London, l. 159. Extensive. One character is led in by another and "set down over the stage in a throne," where he remains for 1700 lines observing and commenting on action below. Although technically this is one continuous appearance "above," his speeches are intermittent and mark thirteen scene divisions.

Massacre at Paris, p. 369. Soldier fires from what has been called a "window." No lines, brief business.

p. 372. Extensive. Terrorists break into the Admiral's "bedroom," murder him in his bed, and pitch his corpse "down" to their leader on the platform below. 10 lines, much business.

The Spanish Tragedy, l. 760. One character places two others in hiding place later said to be "above," from where they observe action below for 55 lines.

l. 1680. One character "at a window" for 15-line soliloquy.

l. 2681. Three characters with royal train enter what has been called a "gallery," from where they observe action below, with some interaction among themselves, for 165 lines.

Tamburlaine, Part 2, p. 204. Four characters with others "upon the walls" speak among themselves for 50 lines, then speak with others below for 15 lines.

p. 206. Forces below "scale the walls." No lines, much business.

p. 209. One character is hung "in chains on the walls." Others shoot him. He hangs there for 75 lines.

Titus Andronicus, I, i. Extensive. Long first scene of over 400 lines uses raised space in conjunction with platform. Tribunes and Senators are "aloft" from the beginning. Then two characters go "up" into the "Senate house," and joint the Tribunes and Senators. Later one of these characters returns "aloft" and has his bride "ascend" to him.

V, ii. One character "opens his study door," speaks to others below, and comes "down" to them. 60 lines.

Troilus and Cressida, plot, l. 15. At least three characters are "on the walls."

l. 47. At least five characters are "on the walls," from which they later "descend."

Woman Will Have her Will, l. 1705. Three characters enter "above" and speak to others below for 75 lines, hoisting one of them halfway to the raised area in a basket.

    l. 1866. Three characters enter, one after another, "above" and speak to others below for 55 lines.

    l. 1999. One character enters "above" and speaks to others below for 35 lines.

    l. 2131. One character enters "above" and speaks to others below for 30 lines.

The significant point can perhaps be seen most clearly in sheer statistics. Only 33 percent of the Rose texts make explicit calls for more than one raised scene, but this group contains 81 percent of all raised scenes in the Rose texts, 90 percent of the speaking characters who appear "above" in the Rose texts, 90 percent of the lines spoken during "above" scenes in the Rose texts, and 100 percent of the scenes which can, in my view, be called "extensive" in the Rose texts. This battery of figures suggests that in about one out of three plays staged at the Rose, some sort of special staging device was used to give raised scenes more stage depth and better visibility than was normally afforded by the permanent structural features of the playhouse, and that for the other two out of three plays the permanent structural features—which probably resembled those shown in the Swan drawing—served well enough. It may always be argued, of course, that all Rose plays, even those with extensive or numerous raised scenes, could have been played from the gallery shown in the Swan drawing. The theatre is capable of gaining its effects in restricted space. To make that argument, however, requires disregarding the division of evidence that has come to light here. Most of the raised scenes at the Rose, including all of the extensive ones, are packed into relatively few of the Rose texts. That division of evidence does not seem to be an accident and should not be ignored.

This impression is deepened by our other consideration. There is a remarkable degree of correspondence between those

Rose texts which call for a special enclosure and those we have just listed as containing more than one explicit indication of raised staging. Here is a list of obvious uses of a special enclosure in the Rose plays (again, page and line references refer to texts cited earlier, in the alphabetical list of Rose plays):

Alphonsus of Aragon, l. 1246. A brazen head is "set in the middle of the place behind the stage," belching flame and oracle.

Battle of Alcazar, plot, l. 27. Three Furies discovered "behind the curtains" in grisly dumb-show.
 l. 84. From "behind the curtains" two characters in a chariot make ceremonial entrance with attendants (Greg's reconstruction).

David and Bethsabe, p. 193. A curtain is drawn and Bethsabe is discovered with her maid, bathing.
 p. 251. David "goes to his pavilion, and sits close a while." Soon "he looks forth, and at the end sits close again." Apparently "close" means the pavilion is closed, for in a moment Joab approaches and "unfolds the pavilion" to reveal David.

Doctor Faustus, Q 1616. Greg parallel text ed., p. 287. "Hell is discovered."

Downfall and Death of Huntington. Downfall, l. 52. Huntington and Maid Marian "sit down within the curtains." Four others, "drawing the curtains," enter and are entertained in dumb-show. "The curtains are again shut."
 l. 85. Above dumb-show repeated, with "the curtains" referred to again.
 l. 1490. "Curtains open, Robin Hood sleeps on a green bank, and Marian is strewing flowers on him."
Death, l. 925. Curtains drawn to reveal the King sleeping in his throne and visited by elaborate dumb-show.

Edward I, p. 124. "The Queen's tent opens, she is discovered in her bed," attended by two characters and visited by two others.
 p. 129. "The Queen's tent opens." She is attended by three characters and visited by five.

p. 134. Musicians sing for the Queen "at her tent."

p. 142. Procession of at least three characters and attendants visits the King "in his tent" and then the Queen in "the chamber."

Jew of Malta, p. 333. "A cauldron discovered" within which Barabas, boiling, speaks his last.

Looking Glass for London, p. 510. "They draw the curtains," shutting Remilia in her "tent." After a blast of thunder and lightning, Rasni "draws the curtains and finds her stroken with thunder, black."

Massacre at Paris, p. 395. A "royal cabinet" contains the throne. It is clear that the "cabinet" is a room separate from the main stage and accessible from it. The Guise enters the main stage and *then* knocks to gain admission to the "cabinet," where action is staged.

Old Fortunatus, p. 138. A curtain is drawn to reveal a casket.

p. 163. "A curtain being drawn, where Andelocia lies sleeping in Agripine's lap. . . ." Scene runs 150 lines, using platform together with enclosed space.

2 Seven Deadly Sins, plot, l. 1. "A tent being placed on the stage for Henry VI, he in it, asleep." The "tent" represents the Tower of London.

Spanish Tragedy, l. 2647. Hieronimo "knocks up the curtain," arranging a discovery space for the corpse of his son. The revelation is made at l. 2780: "shows his dead son."

Tamburlaine, Part II, p. 171. "The arras is drawn and Zenocrate lies in her bed of state," with ten characters in attendance.

p. 191. Two characters issue "from the tent" where a third "sits asleep."

Both examples describe Tamburlaine's "tent of war," which is also used in Part I, although no stage directions mention it explicitly.

Titus Andronicus, I, i. The tomb of the Andronici is used prominently. This is a debatable case. Although the tomb is explicitly mentioned and is opened, and although it ought to be an imposing structure, in fact an ordinary stage door could be used.

Troilus and Cressida, plot, l. 36. A scene with "Achilles in his tent" and five other characters.[4]

It will be observed that eleven of these fifteen texts also appear on the list of plays which call for raised staging more than once apiece. To put it another way, 85 percent of the texts calling for more than one raised scene also call for enclosure staging, and these account for three-fourths of all Rose texts that call for enclosure staging. When enclosure staging is evident, the more extensive raised staging is too. Why should 65 percent of explicit indications for raised *or* enclosure staging be concentrated in 28 percent of the Rose plays? Why should 38 percent of the Rose plays have no reference to raised or enclosure staging at all?

The answer, it seems to me, is that the Rose was decked with special staging spaces for some plays but not for others. If we count the texts with no explicit indications for special staging together with those with just one call for raised staging, about half of the plays require nothing beyond the platform and narrow gallery shown in the Swan drawing. The other half call for curtained space, or enclosed space, or multiple scenes above, or stage depth above—several of these together in many cases—and the possibility that they were fitted up in the Swan arrangement seems to me less convincing than the possibility that they employed removable stage devices that provided raised space sufficient for extensive scenes and enclosed space sufficient for discoveries and the larger interior scenes.

Some of the Rose plays were plain, that is, and some were fancy. If the original *Sir Thomas More* was written for the Rose, it was of the fancy variety. The curtained enclosure explicitly indicated for scene ii and the raised staging explicitly indicated for

4. Both *Friar Bacon and Friar Bungay*, l. 1561 and the Quarto of *The Battle of Alcazar*, l. 37 refer to "curtains," but in each case these appear to be curtains on a bed used as a property. The Quarto of *Alcazar* should not be read in the light of the Plot (which does indicate a discovery space) as these are assumed to represent different productions and possibly different theatres. See footnote 3.

the execution scene appear to figure in the other interior scenes of More's career and in his quelling of the May-Day insurrection. These spaces are used with a sense of design, a sense of giving visual organization to the action. The same kinds of spaces figure explicitly in the fancy Rose plays, suggesting that special staging areas were established for those occasions. The special areas in question could have been provided by a removable pavilion, curtained below for discoveries and interiors, its roof affording ample space above. These are the spaces required again and again in the fancy Rose plays; to imagine them being provided by a single removable stage structure is a kind of economical thinking even more interesting to theatre people than to scholars.

It appears that the two hypotheses I have brought together have survived the test of skepticism and may thereby have gained further plausibility. The staging I have inferred for *Sir Thomas More* is not only reflected in about half of the acknowledged Rose plays but seems to have been accommodated by the kind of pavilion most appropriate to the design of *More*.

Let us take one final look at the repertory of Strange's men in 1592–1593, the period in which we suppose the original *Sir Thomas More* was being composed. This will in effect disregard Rose plays from the Admiral's men and other companies, leaving only plays staged by the company I think was responsible for the original *Sir Thomas More*. This evidence has not come to light before, and I want it to be seen. We can identify nine of the plays Strange's men staged during the two seasons for which Henslowe listed their daily repertory. Six are fancy (*The Jew of Malta, The Spanish Tragedy, A Looking Glass for London, The Massacre at Paris, 2 Seven Deadly Sins*, and *1 Henry VI*). Three are plain (*Orlando Furioso, A Knack to Know a Knave*, and *John of Bordeaux*).[5] Of the sixty-seven performances given by Strange's men of these

---

5. I am counting Henslowe's "Friar Bacon" for Strange's as *John of Bordeaux* although the figures would be the same if it were regarded as Greene's *Friar Bacon*.

plays, fifty-two are of fancy texts. In other words, 78 percent of the performances we can identify in the daily repertory of Strange's men emphasized special staging areas. (It may be that *all* their performances had this emphasis, for the plain texts are merely lacking explicit directions about curtains and raised staging; we are not examining their implied staging here.) Their identifiable repertory, then, strongly indicates that Strange's men specialized in the use of these staging areas at the Rose in 1592–1593. Whether or not they were the only troupe to practice such staging extensively is the kind of question that must await the complete study of company characteristics for which I recognize the need at every turn of my argument. For the moment, it must suffice to say that the kind of staging implied in *Sir Thomas More* was not only practiced by Strange's men at the Rose in the early 1590s, but was practiced by them with a frequency approaching the daily.

7
Hand D

Of the six playhouse writers who contributed to either the original or the revision of *Sir Thomas More,* one has an aura of mystery. This is not Hand A, whose identification as Henry Chettle widens no eyes. Dekker as Hand E and Munday as Hand S can be announced in crowded rooms without thanks. The Hand B– Heywood identification is actually debated with some passion, among two persons I know and two others I have heard of. I am convinced that Hand C was as important as any writer in the group (he copied much of what the others wrote, made useful changes along the way, patched things together with bits of his own—the kind of writer without whom plays do not get performed), but I have been unable to start a conversation on the topic. Hand D is all anyone cares about, and the strange thing is that Hand D is the only one of the *More* playhouse hands that cannot be found in other literary or epistolary manuscripts. That is a small part of the mystery. The larger part is that Hand D bears some resemblance to the hand of a known writer who left fourteen words behind in legal documents. Six of the words

are "William," six are "Shakespeare." (The others are "by me.")
From these scrawled signatures has grown an industry devoted
to proving that Hand D's three pages bear the marks of the
Bard.

We are verging on the deferred topic of authorship. Repres-
sions eventually make themselves felt, and the identity of Hand
D is no exception. At the return of the repressed, we must stand
our ground and not give way to anxieties about identity. Angels
and ministers of grace need not defend us if we can avoid questions of identity and instead ask questions about work. The
pages of writing in Hand D were intended to do a certain kind of
work, and that work has not been regarded very closely. The
persistent anxiety about his identity has blocked it from view.

Hand D has usually been taken as one of the revisers of the
play. The three pages in his handwriting, folios 8a, 8b, and 9a,
form the bulk of Addition II, which also has contributions from
Hands B and C and is fitted as a five-page unit into the original.
Nothing could seem more natural to a reader than that Hand D
was part of a team of revisers who more or less worked together.

The theatre is deceptive when it comes to making things seem
natural, however. Theatre people like to fit disparate things
together so that they seem to have grown that way, but they
haven't grown that way, they have been fitted. The purpose of
Hand C's skill at fitting things was to make the seams invisible in
the final product. This play of *More*, written by six men probably
over a gap of ten years, should with a little suspension of dis-
belief strike an audience in the theatre as being natural.

Let us take a close look at Hand D's three pages. They do not
grow naturally out of the preceding material. They have been
carefully fitted. Thanks to C, who did the fitting, D's section
seems to begin a new scene, with the leader of the uprising, John
Lincoln, quieting the crowd: "Peace heare me" (Addition II, l.
122). Yet D did not write an entrance direction for this scene.
The entrance direction is in Hand C, and it appears at the bottom of the previous page. If D was beginning a new scene on a
new page, why did he not write his own entrance direction at the

top of the page? It appears that Hand C, in writing the entrance direction at the bottom of the preceding page, was joining up with writing already done by D. Lincoln's "Peace heare me" could very well have been originally written as part of a scene in progress, in which case some of D's writing has been removed in favor of cutting in on a new opening. That would explain why no entrance direction appears by Hand D and why C wrote the entrance direction at the bottom of the preceding page. It would also explain why C's entrance direction makes a distinction between the Clown and George Betts which seems to have been unknown to D; this matter will be discussed in a moment.

Is there any other evidence of a separation between Hand D and the revisers? The possibility is that D worked on an earlier stage of the composition, and may have been one of the original writers. As it happens, there is further evidence, although in setting it forward I must take some liberties with the one writer of this manuscript who has become hallowed with mystery. When one looks at what Hand D actually wrote, one discovers that he was unaware of some things. He did not know what the other revisers were doing, for example, and he did not know what the censor had done. I propose to examine the things Hand D did not know, for I think they tell us something new about his role in the composition of the play.

The value of taking a fresh look at what Hand D actually wrote has been demonstrated by Peter Blayney, who has noticed something about our author which had been forgotten since 1844. On the verso of folio 9, which everyone since Dyce had been saying was blank, Blayney found one more word written by D: "all."[1] Apparently Hand D turned over the page and was beginning to write more dialogue when it came to his attention that there was no need to continue. In taking up the question of what Hand D did not know, I am glad to borrow the first point

---

1. Peter Blayney, "*The Booke of Sir Thomas Moore* Re-examined," *Studies in Philology*, 69 (1972), 168. An outstanding bibliographical guide to the authorship controversy is G. Harold Metz, *Four Plays Ascribed to Shakespeare* (New York: Garland, 1982).

from Blayney and note that Hand D did not know where to stop. Or else, to add a possibility to Blayney's interpretation, he did not know where to start. Since the first word on the fully written side of folio 9 is also "all," D might have made a false beginning and then turned the page over.

What else did Hand D not know? When Edmund Tilney, the Master of the Revels, wrote his general censorship at the beginning of the manuscript, he insisted that the Ill May-Day uprising be narrated rather than dramatized and that the narration use the word "Lombards" for the foreigners against whom the uprising was directed. That is what Tilney plainly meant when he said "Leave out ye insurrection wholy," and required it to be replaced with "a shortt reportt" of Sir Thomas More's good service in putting down a mutiny "agaynst ye Lumbards only." He specified "Lombards" because he disliked the word "strangers." There are seventeen instances of the word "strangers" in the manuscript that Tilney censored, and fourteen of them are in passages marked for deletion (not always by Tilney). At one point (l. 365) Tilney even crossed out the offending word and interlined "Lombard." A few lines further on, he replaced "Frenchman" with "Lombard." Clearly Tilney wanted the foreigners to be called "Lombards," and the word that was to be eradicated was "stranger."

Hand D was oblivious to Tilney's censorship. He was dramatizing one of the events Tilney wanted to have narrated (in fact, the event Tilney actually named, for Hand D showed the good service More did in quelling the mutiny), and he used "strangers" seven times. Indeed, More's clever rhetoric turns on the very word, for in asking the rioters to imagine themselves in another country and suffering mistreatment, he tells them they would be "strangers" too. Either Hand D wrote so long after Tilney's censorship that he could disregard it, or he wrote before Tilney's censorship and could not have seen it. Both are real possibilities, but the balance will tip, I believe, in favor of Hand D's early writing.

For Hand D also did not know some things that the revisers were doing. The revisers were removing a group of characters from the uprising scenes, for example. The apprentices, who in the original version joined the mutiny after having wounded a chiding authority, Sir John Munday, have been entirely removed from the revised version. Their scene with Munday has been cut, and so has the wounded Munday's report of their behavior in Addition II. In fact, Munday's role has been entirely eliminated too. These are the cuts which I have suggested in Chapter 3 were made for purposes of reducing a large play to normal casting. The point is that Hand D thought that the apprentices were still involved in the uprising. In his scene, the rabble-rousing John Lincoln harps on the injustices done to apprentices. At line 132 it is the apprentices who are being "undone" by the customs of the foreigners, and when the Sergeant at Arms accuses the crowd of being "simple," they turn on him for calling apprentices simple (modernized text):

Sergeant.	You are the simplest things that ever stood in such a question.
Lincoln.	How say you now? Prentices simple! down with him!
All.	Prentices simple, prentices simple! [Add. II, ll. 143–145]

There is no reason for this emphasis on apprentices after the cuts have been made. It would appear that the conclusion is clear: Hand D did not know the cuts had been made. He wrote with the original apprentice scene in mind.

Moreover, it is clear—but not to Hand D—that one of the revisers was mainly engaged in building up a Clown's role in the insurrection. The new role was being created by Hand B out of one of the two brothers named Betts who were paired in the original insurrection. The original intentions can be seen in the opening episode, where line 63 (by Hand S) makes certain that two brothers Betts are onstage. That Hand B was later turning one of the brothers into the Clown's role is apparent at line 4 of Addition II, where George Betts reacts to the "Clown" as his "brother." This distinction between George Betts and "Clown Betts" in the revised play was not apparent to Hand D, who has speeches for only one of the two and calls him simply "Betts" (when he is not calling him "other"). Hand C has come along at a later stage to assign some of these speeches to George Betts and some to "Betts Clown," thus insisting on a distinction of which D must have been unaware. It is sometimes asserted that Hand D was careless about all the rebels' names, but this is not exactly true. His early lines do resort to "other" when someone besides the leader, John Lincoln, is speaking, but as the scene progresses, Hand D becomes more specific about the other rebels, and distinguishes among Lincoln, Doll, Sherwin, and Betts. But he does not distinguish between the two Bettses. It looks as though he did not know that a role for the Clown was being added to the play.

Our examples of what Hand D did not know are parallel to one another and indicate that he worked in advance of the revisions by Hands B and C, and probably in advance of the censorship by Tilney. There is another possibility, to be sure. Hand D may have been a little bit incompetent. This view has recently been advanced by Giorgio Melchiori, who in the face of all the piety that has been bestowed on the Shakespearean possibility adopts the refreshing attitude that Hand D did not know what the rest of the play was about.[2] He was revising carelessly and managed to ruin the uprising scenes in his haste. Munday had portrayed the English craftsmen in the sympathetic and even heroic light, according to this reading, but Hand D turned them into a fickle and foolish mob. Melchiori does not draw together the particular points we have noticed about what Hand D did not know, but they would be subsumed under his general theory of bad playwrighting.

Yet Hand D was alert to a deliberate and gradual shift of emphasis in the rebellion scenes, and far from appearing incom-

2. In an essay to be included in a forthcoming collection of new commentary on *Sir Thomas More*, ed. T. H. Howard-Hill. I am indebted to Professors Melchiori and Howard-Hill for making this essay available to me in advance of publication. See also Melchiori, "Hand D in *Sir Thomas More:* An Essay in Misinterpretation," *Shakespeare Survey*, 38 (1985), 101–114.

petent, he seems to me observant of the dynamics of the play and able to exploit them shrewdly. It is true, as Melchiori argues, that the English craftsmen have decency and reasonableness on their side in the first scene. They have been outraged by arrogant and high-handed foreigners. In the second scene, however, which was also written by Munday, a change begins to occur in the direction of mob hysteria. These artisans have decided to take the law into their own hands: they will be the "rough Ministers of law" and their "justice" consists of setting fire to the houses of the foreigners.

What Hand D does in writing the third scene of insurrection is to show another increase of xenophobia among the rioters. This is an abrupt intensification of a shift which began in the second scene's presentation of the crowd. Hand D knew that Munday was dramatizing what happens to crowds when they take to the streets in rage (even in well-justified rage), and he was carrying the dramatization a large step further.

Moreover, Hand D shows clear awareness of the crowd's original decency. The extraordinary thing about his wild-eyed mob is that once the effective figure of authority stands before them, they are prepared to listen and even to return to the decency and reasonableness they displayed in the beginning. Hand D certainly knows how they were portrayed in the opening scene. In this respect they differ sharply from the mob to which they are most often compared—Jack Cade's followers in 2 *Henry VI*. Cade's followers cannot listen to reason. They are like the feather blown in the wind, reacting mindlessly to whatever influence is brought to bear on them. The crowd in *Sir Thomas More* listens to reason—reason as Hand D articulated it for the hero, in any event—and agrees to submit to the King's mercy. Scholars may well feel that the dramatist of the Jack Cade scenes must be the same as Hand D, but these are widely different crowds. And in showing his awareness of the reasonableness of the crowd in the opening scene, Hand D is doing just what he did in showing his awareness of the increasing hysteria of the crowd in the second scene: he is writing professionally, with full knowledge of how this play was developing. Thus, although Melchiori stands among the steadfast in refusing to quail before Hand D's identity, I cannot agree with him that the playwright was a professional incompetent. Hand D seems, on the contrary, to have been fully aware of the earlier crowd scenes and capable of building on them.

Let us be exact about what Hand D did and did not know. He did know how the original play was developing. He did not know (or did not care) what Tilney wrote on the original manuscript, he did not know that the apprentices were revised out of the play, and he did not know that the Clown was revised into the play as Betts's brother. These are the sorts of things professional playwrights have to know about once they have happened, and Hand D has to be recognized as a professional.

There are two possible interpretations. One is that Hand D participated in the original composition of the play, as a collaborator with Hand S (and other writers, perhaps, for S may have copied lines which originated with others). The other is that although Hand D came to the manuscript at a later stage, as a reviser, he worked ahead of B and C and thus did not know of the changes they introduced and did not care about Tilney's strictures. The first interpretation would place D's writing in the early 1590s, according to our dating, while the other would have to be rather vague about the date of his work, placing it sometime prior to the revisions of B and C in 1603 or later.

Let us examine the second interpretation more closely. It explains D's lack of awareness of the other revisers' work by placing his writing earlier than theirs. It does not explain why one reviser would be out of step with the others, and thus leaves hanging what is so often left hanging in discussions of this manuscript, the implication that professional writers botched the job. I have taken pains to show that the manuscript does not represent a botched job in other respects. It has been finished to the point where actors' parts can be copied, it has been revised for the sake of effective casting and staging. There is no ground for using the botched-job hypothesis to explain any feature of the manuscript that can be explained by another hypothesis.

The first interpretation, which assumes that professional writers did their work coherently, seems to me preferable. It accounts for all the evidence accounted for in the second interpretation, and does not leave hanging the question of why one reviser would be out of step with the others. If D was one of the writers of the original version, the things he did not know are all explained by one reason: his writing preceded all the interventions—the intervention of the censor as well as those of the later revisers.

I know of only one objection that can be raised to this interpretation, and I believe it is groundless. It has often been claimed that Hand D's three pages cannot have belonged to the original manuscript submitted to Tilney, because Tilney made no marks on those three pages. As we noted earlier, however, Tilney marked very few of the pages that everyone agrees were submitted to him, the pages in Hand S. On only three of the undisputed original pages did Greg detect Tilney's hand: folios 3a, 5a, and 17b. It is often assumed that other marks in the manuscript came from Tilney, but his hand has not been demonstrated apart from the three pages mentioned.[3] The other deletions either belong to the known playhouse revisers or have not been identified. In other words, Tilney's censorship was highly selective until he wrote the general strictures at the beginning of the first scene. If he did not leave his mark on twenty-two of the twenty-five pages in Hand S, it is not at all surprising that he did not leave his mark on any of the three pages in Hand D. Much of Hand D's writing would have pleased the royal censor anyhow. The writer who showed a riot being brought to order by a persuasive official is the sort of writer who would

3. I follow Greg's analysis in the introduction and notes to his Malone Society Reprint. R. C. Bald also found Tilney's hand in only three scenes. See Bald, "*The Booke of Sir Thomas More* and Its Problems," *Shakespeare Survey*, 2 (1949), 50. G. Melchiori, *Shakespeare Quarterly*, 37 (1986), p. 294 adds fol. 10.

have found favor at court. That Hand D used the offensive word "stranger" without having it censored by Tilney causes no problems. Tilney's specific marks against the word do not occur after folio 5a, several pages before D's section begins. It seems obvious that Tilney stopped pursuing individual instances of the offensive word on folio 5a, and resorted instead to the general note at the beginning about using Lombards. Twice "stranger" is allowed to stand on folio 11a, and that page was certainly submitted.

On balance, then, the evidence demonstrates that Hand D worked ahead of the revisionary efforts of Hands B and C, and although it remains possible that he worked *just* ahead of them, as a reviser one jump ahead of other revisers (the group being careless about fitting the pieces together, not caring that one of their number was counting on apprentices whom the others were cutting, not caring that one of their number did not know that a Clown's role was being sharpened out of the shadowy Brother Betts), the clearer explanation is that Hand D did not belong to the group of revisers at all, but was one of the composers of the original play. Let us note the implications that follow from the clearer explanation. Hand D's three pages have always been recognized as "foul papers"—that is, pages of first-draft writing which turned out to be usable without copying. Nearly all the rest of the original version is in the hand of Anthony Munday, who is thought to have been sometimes authoring his own text and sometimes copying the text of others. One implication is that Hand D may have written other portions of the original play, portions which Munday copied.[4] Those who pursue the identity of Hand D may enjoy spotting the passages that sound like their man. But touchstones are not my concern here. I merely note the possibility that Hand D participated

---

4. See E. H. C. Oliphant, "Sir Thomas More," *Journal of English and Germanic Philology*, 18 (1919), 226–235; Bald, "*The Booke of Sir Thomas More* and Its Problems," p. 47; Blayney, "*The Booke of Sir Thomas Moore* Re-examined," p. 172n.

more extensively in the original play than the three pages in his hand would indicate.

If Munday and Hand D were working together in some way on the original, was anyone else part of the collaboration? There is a good possibility that Hand A, whose identification as Henry Chettle is no longer in question, was another of the original dramatists. His one page of writing (folio 6a) is a revision of lines in Munday's hand, but this kind of rewriting can just as plausibly be assigned to the original composition as to the later revision. When writers collaborate, some dovetailing, adjustment, and rewriting always occurs. Collaboration is normally done that way. What Peter Blayney noticed about Hand D—that he did not know exactly where to stop and was preparing to continue writing on the verso of folio 9—suggests that he was rewriting a passage of Munday's and was about to miss the mark of the join, but this no more proves him a later reviser than an original collaborator. The political motive that has been detected behind Chettle's stint of rewriting would have been appropriate at any point in the transmission of the text. The theatrical purposes of casting and staging which we have identified in the later revision involve only Hands B, C, and E. Chettle cannot be shown to have written any undeniably later Additions, and in that respect he joins Munday and Hand D, all of whom seem to have been untroubled by the unusually large cast required by the original play. The question for Chettle cannot be settled either way, but the possibility is clear that he, like Hand D, was one of the original authors, and that both of them did some supplemental writing which was left uncopied by Munday.

Let us pursue the possibility that Munday, Chettle, and Hand D were among the original writers of *Sir Thomas More*. They may have had help from Hand C, who seems to have been active in both the original and the later revision, but Hand B and Dekker have always been taken as revisers only, and our discussion of the purposes behind their work does not change that designation. Does this division of labor make sense in view of other evidence?

We know something about the ages of Chettle, Munday, Dekker, and (with a reminder that he is a questionable identity for
Hand B) Heywood. Chettle and Munday were about ten years
older than Dekker and Heywood. According to my hypothesis
from Chapter 3, the original version was written for Lord
Strange's men in the early 1590s. Munday and Chettle were at
that time both in their early thirties. Munday is known to have
written plays by then, and Chettle, who was a writer and printer
acquainted with various theatre people, had probably written
plays too. Both were regularly in the employ of the Henslowe-
Alleyn companies after 1594. Hand C, as I have noted earlier,
was associated with the Henslowe-Alleyn companies too, and can
be connected with Strange's men through his writing of the
"plot" of 2 *Seven Deadly Sins*.

The younger writers, Dekker and Heywood, cannot be shown
to have established themselves as London playwrights until the
second half of the 1590s. Both were active writers for the
Henslowe-Alleyn companies into the early years of the new century, when I hold that the revision of the play was prepared for
the Admiral's men.

My assumption about the division of labor would be undercut
by evidence that the presumed earlier group knew the work of
the presumed later group on this manuscript. This cannot be
shown, and some evidence that I do not believe has been discussed before points the other way. The earlier group does not
overwrite the later group. I am talking about actual writing done
on actual paper. The earlier group writes on pages that were
blank to begin with. The later group sometimes writes on blank
pages and sometimes overwrites the writing of others. Hand B
writes on folios 10a, 10b, and 11a, already in Munday's hand.
Hand C writes on many pages, including some in Munday's
hand, some in Hand B, some in Hand D. Dekker writes on folio
13b, already in Hand C. Such overwriting is an obvious sign of
patching and tinkering, and no certain sign of this sort comes
from Munday, Chettle, and Hand D. We must disregard some
marginalia and alterations which cannot be assigned to any writ-

er and restrict ourselves to the 99 percent of the text that can be attributed, but within those confines our earlier group writes only on pages originated by themselves and shows no awareness of the writing done by the later group.[5]

The possibility that Hand D collaborated with Munday and Chettle in the 1590s has recently received corroboration from one of Peter Blayney's stimulating pieces of detective work.[6] Blayney has found signs that Hand D's section of *Sir Thomas More* had such an impact on Chettle that when Chettle wrote *Kind-Heart's Dream* in late 1592, he incorporated little bursts of echo from this influential author. These echoes occurred on a "less-than-conscious level," Blayney speculates, and he warns us to regard them cautiously. That is, I submit, how one should regard everything about Hand D, who appears to have been a bit ghostly even in his own time, insinuating his word into the book and volume of Henry Chettle's brain. *Kind-Heart's Dream* is a ghost story in its own right, come to think of it. It has five ghosts, not counting Hand D.

Who might have been writing plays with Chettle and Munday in the early 1590s? for Lord Strange's men? with such impact as to leave a mark on Chettle's unconscious? We are tracing the possibilities for Hand D, seeing if the tracings make a pattern within which he can be laid to rest.

Let us take Lord Strange's men first. E. K. Chambers' analysis of their repertory names Marlowe, Greene, Lodge, Peele, Kyd,

5. For attributions I follow W. W. Greg, "The Handwritings of the Manuscript," in A. W. Pollard, ed., *Shakespeare's Hand in the Play of Sir Thomas More* (Cambridge: Cambridge Univ. Press, 1923), pp. 41–56, along with Greg's review in *The Library*, 4th ser., 9 (1928–1929) of S. A. Tannenbaum's *The Booke of Sir Thomas More: A Bibliotic Study* (New York: privately printed, 1927). Blayney, "*The Booke of Sir Thomas Moore* Re-examined," p. 171n., detects the marks of a left-handed reviser on various pages and thinks that Chettle was the only lefthanded writer involved. I have not included these sinister marks among the accepted attributions, but they would have the effect of placing Chettle among the later revisers. That would not preclude him from the original composition, of course, but it would reduce the group who did not overwrite the pages of others to Munday and Hand D.

6. Blayney, "*The Booke of Sir Thomas Moore* Re-examined," pp. 182–189.

and Shakespeare as authors whose plays can reasonably be identified in Henslowe's lists for 19 February to 22 June 1592 and 29 December 1592 to 1 February 1593.[7] I take the liberty of adding Chettle, on the argument I have advanced elsewhere that the manuscript *John of Bordeaux* (which has some lines in Chettle's hand) represents the play Henslowe called *Friar Bacon* for Strange's men.[8] The plays that can be attributed to these writers constitute less than one-third of the titles in Henslowe's lists for Strange's men, but they do give us some names to consider.

From four of these writers, sufficient holograph samples remain to assure that an identification with Hand D is impossible: Lodge, Peele, Kyd, and Chettle (thus eliminating the possibility that Chettle was influencing himself in *Kind-Heart's Dream*). That leaves Marlowe, Greene, and Shakespeare. Oddly, these appear to be the very writers alluded to by Chettle in his prefatory letter to *Kind-Heart's Dream,* which mentions Greene's attack on two dramatists who are usually thought to be Marlowe and Shakespeare.

Let us consider Marlowe as Hand D, strange as the idea may seem. Marlowe has been the subject of some paleographical examination. He was long conjectured to have been the writer of the *"Massacre at Paris* leaf," now at the Folger Library, but as the experts gradually allowed themselves to be informed that a Marlowe signature had been found in 1939 and that it fails to resemble the writing on the *"Massacre* leaf," this notion has been abandoned. We have only Marlowe's one signature, which does not resemble Hand D very closely, although the evidence is really too slight to permit a conclusion one way or the other. I suspect that Marlowe has never been considered a candidate for Hand D because no one is willing to believe that he could have written at such length in favor of obedience. This is not a good reason to exclude him, but neither can it be denied. It may be noted that

---

7. Chambers, *The Elizabethan Stage* (Oxford: Clarendon Press, 1923), II, 122–123.

8. "The Ownership of *The Jew of Malta, Friar Bacon,* and *The Ranger's Comedy,*" *English Language Notes,* 9 (1972), 249–252.

Chettle disliked Marlowe. But writers can be influenced, perhaps especially, by those they hate. I find it more telling that Chettle hopes he will never make the acquaintance of this dislikable writer, for he is unlikely to have collaborated with a man he never met.

Greene is a stronger candidate. He left no manuscripts behind to trouble us, was capable of stretching for eloquence from *any* point of view, and was a friend of Chettle's. If phrases by Hand D were circulating in Chettle's mind when he wrote *Kind-Heart's Dream,* it is not hard to imagine Greene as the source. Chettle had edited some of Greene's work. He wished he had edited a bit more, but still there was a literary relationship. Greene is even a character in *Kind-Heart's Dream.* He is one of the ghosts. We always seem to be dealing with ghosts when troubling over an author's identity.

Then there is Shakespeare. We are venturing onto the battlements now. For although Shakespeare is not a ghost in *Kind-Heart's Dream,* he does seem to be mentioned with admiration.[9] That is, the prefatory letter which discusses Greene and two other dramatists praises one of those dramatists, the one who is not dislikable, for civil demeanor and facetious grace in writing. It does appear that Chettle's playwright of quick pen and trusty brow was Shakespeare. If so, Chettle tells us when he met Shakespeare—between September and December of 1592, during the span of time in which we have placed the original writing of *Sir Thomas More* for Strange's men.

In other words, if we put Blayney's reasoning together with our evidence about the date and company of the original version, a story can be told which recounts some of the things Shakespeare was doing in the fall of 1592. He was working with Chettle and Munday on a new play for Strange's men, having

---

9. I follow Harold Jenkins, *The Life and Work of Henry Chettle* (London: Sedgewick and Jackson, 1934), p. 10, for identifications of Shakespeare and Marlowe in the prefatory letter to *Kind-Heart's Dream.* See also E. K. Chambers, *William Shakespeare: A Study of Facts and Problems* (Oxford: Clarendon Press, 1930), I, 58–59.

been responsible for at least one of that company's successes, a play on the reign of Henry VI, a few months before. The theatres were closed at the time, perhaps because of the plague, perhaps also because of the Southwark riot of the previous June, and Strange's men, complaining that they were too large a company to travel, were waiting for the Rose to reopen. Chettle, Munday, and Shakespeare were writing a history play that would use the resources of this large company to the full, would provide another dominant role for Alleyn, and would, not incidentally, dramatize a riot on the very problem of anti-alien resentment that was then threatening violence in London. (Marlowe was also writing a new play on a politically dangerous topic for Strange's men in *The Massacre at Paris*.) The scene in which More quiets the crowd of artisans and convinces them to accept the King's mercy was so powerfully written by Shakespeare—who was strengthening that scene, dovetailing a better speech into the place of a weaker speech—that Chettle's own writing of later that fall, *Kind-Heart's Dream*, echoed its language in clusters. The Master of the Revels, less impressed than Chettle, refused to license the manuscript unless major changes were made, including the elimination of the very scene that Chettle liked especially. Of no period in Shakespeare's artistic career can such a specific story be told. And it depends not a jot on the evidence of handwriting. The similarity between the Shakespeare signatures and the pages by Hand D would only support the identification on which this eventful story rests.

And the story is almost bound to be untrue. Its every element is hedged with doubt. There is no direct evidence that Chettle and Munday were writing for Strange's men before 1594. Chettle does not name Shakespeare in *Kind-Heart's Dream*. The evidence that Chettle was influenced by Hand D has to be regarded with caution—a similarity of phrasing between two works often occurs because of a generally shared linguistic currency rather than a "borrowing" by one author from another. There are differences between Hand D and the Shakespeare signatures. Our new hypotheses about the date and company of the original play have carried the warning that theatrical characteristics of other companies must be studied before the theatrical characteristics of Strange's men can be seen in context. The story amounts to one hypothesis stacked on another and will not carry much weight.

The point to examine is how stories come into being in the first place. It is true that a story takes shape on the naming of Hand D as Shakespeare, a better story than is set in motion by the name of Marlowe or Greene or any other identifiable dramatist. The ghost I was keeping at bay on the margins threatens to loom up as the Bard after all. But I also have to admit that the desire to tell a story is deceptive. It links elements which are doubtful, turning possibilities in upon one another so that they appear to be the factual occasions for narrative to build upon, when what is really occurring, at the heart of every narrative, is the demonstration of identity for dead or absent persons.

Here are two stories about the dead person who threatens Hand D with his name: Shakespeare. They are really anecdotes, but I offer them on the assumption that an anecdote is a stripped-down narrative in which the core of storytelling can be seen. They are two anecdotes telling how Sir Edward Maunde Thompson, the most famous English paleographer of his time, was convinced that Hand D was Shakespeare. Both versions say that Sir Edward made his discovery late in life, after having served as Keeper of Manuscripts and then Principal Librarian at the British Museum, and they agree on the gentle irony that this venerable man was making his discovery in a manuscript that had been in his official keeping for many years. Then the versions differ. One comes from A. W. Pollard in 1923: "After an exhaustive study of the manuscript he became convinced that here he was in truth confronted with a holograph literary manuscript of our greatest English poet."[10] The other comes from J. Dover Wilson in 1956, who said that when Thompson took down the *More* manuscript from the shelf and opened it to the

10. Pollard, ed., *Shakespeare's Hand in the Play of Sir Thomas More*, p. 11.

pages by Hand D, "he threw up his hands and cried 'Shake-speare!'"[11] So the "Eureka" version exists alongside the "exhaustive study" version, the matter being complicated by Wilson's recollection that he heard the "Eureka" version from Pollard, who wrote the "exhaustive study" version himself.

Thus, while it may very well be true that Shakespeare was Hand D, I prefer to conclude in the area of doubt where names do not flow so easily and where stories are harder to tell. Earlier I noted that two-thirds of the plays performed by Strange's men at the Rose cannot be attributed to a known Elizabethan playwright. We do not know who wrote *Mulomurco, The Spanish Comedy, Sir John Mandeville, Pope Joan*—the list runs to considerable length, and the odds are favorable that if Hand D wrote some of *Sir Thomas More* for this repertory, he wrote some of these other plays too.

No name was available for the authors of these unattributable Rose plays until 1940, when Virginia Woolf realized that they were all written by Anon and that Anon could be described.[12] He was the leading playwright in London from the establishment of the permanent theatre in 1576 until the emergence of printed plays which carried their authors' names. Working from Greg's edition of Henslowe's *Diary*, Woolf saw that Anon was a major writer for Strange's men at the Rose and that he was there engaged with the very writers who would eventually eclipse him, writers such as Marlowe, Kyd, and Shakespeare. In describing *Sir Thomas More* as a play intended for this repertory, we are locating it at the scene of a cultural battle between Anon and the others.

Woolf's story attracts me because it gains its impulse from a name free of identity. She knew the characteristics of Anon, but not his identity. Indeed, "his" should not be said (for Anon is

11. J. Dover Wilson, "The New Way with Shakespeare's Texts, III," *Shakespeare Survey*, 9 (1956), 73.

12. It was another thirty years before Woolf's essay was published. See Brenda R. Silver, "'Anon' and 'The Reader': Virginia Woolf's Last Essays," *Twentieth Century Literature*, 25 (1979), 356–441.

female too). Anon was created by the audience. He was writing their language for them, reflecting their idiom, giving them plots which they gathered to see. Marlowe, Kyd, and Shakespeare destroyed that relationship by writing an individualized language that rattled the gatherings and made the spectators see the power of singularity on the stage.

Only one of Anon's many plays for Strange's men at the Rose got into print: *A Knack to Know a Knave*. This can be read against the three pages by Hand D as a way of determining if Anon is the name of our ghostly author, but the test will result in an ambiguity that even Woolf (who brilliantly noted that ambiguity is Anon's trademark—I am much indebted to her here) did not heed. Hand D's scene sets the formal rhetoric of the hero against the prose outbursts of an outraged crowd, and the ambiguity is that Hand D sounds like Anon when he writes for the crowd and like Shakespeare (to choose a name) when he writes for the hero. There are even touches of Shakespeare in the crowd, touches of Anon in the hero. These three pages tend to blend Anon into Shakespeare, and although all readers will want to make these discriminations for themselves, the conclusion is before us and must be seized. Hand D will be found in a writer who is both ordinary and exceptional, able to reflect common speech and to produce singularity, Anon and Shakespeare at once.

It is at this point that the discipline of paleography presents a further possibility for Hand D. In an oft-quoted paragraph about paleographical evidence Greg said that aside from Shakespeare, "it can be shown that D was not written by any dramatist of whose hand we have adequate knowledge."[13] This has proved to be an influential statement. It has not, however, proved to be true.

Greg was excluding from consideration the one dramatic writer whose hand resembles that of Hand D closely enough to deserve attention. Indeed, this identification was generally taken

13. W. W. Greg, *Collected Papers*, ed. J. C. Maxwell (Oxford: Clarendon Press, 1966), p. 200.

for granted before Greg's edition of 1911 dismissed it out of hand. In 1975 it was again mentioned by Michael Hays, and it has most recently been set forward by Anthony Petti, in his *English Literary Hands from Chaucer to Dryden,* who notes that the hand in question might be Hand D's written somewhat later.[14]

Who is this candidate for Hand D? And how can Greg have missed seeing his hand? To the second question the answer is that Greg did not miss seeing his hand at all, and may well have been the scholar who studied it most often. It is, for one thing, a prominent hand in *The Book of Sir Thomas More.* What Greg overlooked was not the hand itself but the fact that the hand belonged to a dramatist. For it is Hand C that bears a resemblance to Hand D, our very own Hand C, who worked over various parts of the manuscript, stitching together passages from the others, copying their work (or was it his own?), correcting some stage directions, and getting the thing into shape for the actors to work on. He was in touch with Anon as well as with Shakespeare, in position to blend elements of their styles. But Greg never thought of Hand C as a "dramatist." He was a "playhouse functionary." The model that produces this distinction is the model of literary canonization, which gives the privilege of genius to authors and holds those responsible for the material conditions of literature—actors, for example, but also printers, scribes, stationers, and paper manufacturers, just to name those whose work Shakespeare would have valued—as more or less contemptible.

I am far from certain that Hand C was Hand D, but the possibility brings me joy. After all the solemnity that has over the generations gone into proving that Hand D was Shakespeare, a possibility that the present study has not dislodged and may even have furthered, I cannot discountenance the idea that

---

14. Michael Hays, "Watermarks in the Manuscript of *Sir Thomas More* and a Possible Collation," *Shakespeare Quarterly,* 26 (1975), 66–69. Anthony Petti, *English Literary Hands from Chaucer to Dryden* (Cambridge: Harvard Univ. Press, 1977), p. 91.

Hand C was joined to this mysterious body. Here is the careful statement from Anthony Petti's *English Literary Hands from Chaucer to Dryden:*

> Hand C may be that of a leading dramatist, and the resemblance it bears to Hand D . . . should not be completely ignored, since it has most of the same minuscule graphs, though its spurred *a* lacks the "crucial" horizontal continuation of the descender (except perhaps in l. 29, *hange*) and final *f* has a reversed *c* finial rather than the dangling Greek *e* of Hand D's *f*. The apparent revision of Hand C [at Add. II, l. 237] might be Hand D's written somewhat later. [P. 91]

Doubts will spring to the minds of Shakespeareans everywhere. How could an author have misunderstood his own passage "somewhat later" (at l. 237) where a problem caused only by the absence of punctuation has been solved by crossing out three lines and replacing them with the pedantic "tell me but this"? Such an author would have to be working at odds with himself. Sir Edward Maunde Thompson could *see* that Hand D was not working at odds with himself. Hand D was very closely in touch with his moods as he wrote. He rippled along through his first two pages, as Sir Edward could plainly see from the marks on the pages, then as he came to the philosophical part of More's address to the crowd he became pensive and applied thoughtful pressure to his pen. How did Sir Edward put it? This writing was "of an unusual fluency which could respond instantaneously to the moods of the writer."[15]

How did Hemings and Condell put it? "His mind and hand went together: and what he thought, he uttered with that easiness, that we have scarce received from him a blot in his papers." I quote from their preface to the Folio of 1623, which contains, I believe, the first effort to account for this author by means of his handwriting. The Shakespeare known to Hemings and Condell blends nicely with Sir Edward's scientific description of Hand D,

---

15. Pollard, ed., *Shakespeare's Hand in the Play of Sir Thomas More*, pp. 69–70.

so nicely that one wonders if a trace of literary influence might be detected here, but the point is that, call him what we will, Shakespeare or Hand D, a writer of such unblotted fluency can scarcely be held responsible for the serviceable and unrefined patchwork writing of Hand C.

Yet I have stumbled over enough garbled passages in the printed works of Shakespeare to make me certain that the compositors were dealing with blotted papers. Someone like Hand C must have worked often with our author, perhaps helping him with all of the minute revisions of his own works which are postulated in the newest bibliographical studies.[16] And if Shakespeare did revise, perhaps he was at odds with himself after all. It is easier to think that Hand C was at odds with Hand D than that Hand D was at odds with himself, but the similarity of handwriting between them reminds us that every author is his own blotter to some extent.

How did the experts decide that Hand C was not the same as Hand D? Greg announced their difference in his 1911 edition with one sentence: Hand D "is certainly a different hand from C, with which it has been sometimes confused, but C is found correcting it rather freely" (p. ix). There is no demonstration of the difference, just the assertion. Greg was entirely consistent in this regard: in both of his later major pronouncements on the *More* handwriting, he scrupulously remarked that Hands C and D were once thought to be the same, but that the weight of paleographical evidence was now against this view.[17] Exactly what that paleographical evidence amounts to remains unstated. The last of Greg's statements on the question, in "Shakespeare's Hand Once More," says that he agrees with Sir Edward on this point, but Sir Edward's three major publications on the *More*

16. The leading example is *King Lear;* for a convenient sampling, see Gary Taylor and Michael Warren, eds., *The Division of the Kingdom* (Oxford: Clarendon Press, 1983).
17. See Greg, "The Handwritings of the Manuscript," in Pollard, ed., *Shakespeare's Hand in the Play of Sir Thomas More*, p. 46, and "Shakespeare's Hand Once More" in Greg, *Collected Papers*, p. 193.

writers contain only one mention of Hand C's paleographical characteristics, and that is offered as a *similarity* to Hand D.[18] Sir Edward may have told Sir Walter over tea or a brandy, but he didn't put it in print.

Not the handwriting but the experts are the most interesting topic here. For some reason a difference between C and D hardens into fact without being described. Only Anthony Petti, among the experts I have read, offers any description of the evidence, and he raises the possibility that C and D were the same. I have looked at them both and see similarities along with differences. I have looked at the Shakespeare signatures and Hand D: similarities and differences again. My own handwriting always looks the same to me, but I asked someone to look at samples written a year apart: similarities and differences—very slight differences, I hasten to add. The experts who established the difference between C and D were certain they saw a real distinction, but they were also certain of another difference between C and D. They were certain that D was a playwright and C was a functionary. Moreover, they became certain, if only after patient study, that the playwright was Shakespeare. Thus the distinction between playwright and functionary became tinged with the distinction between genius and scribe, and this resembles the distinction between master and slave. Here is Greg on the passage which Petti described in the quotation I gave earlier. Greg writes in the full confidence that D and C were different, that one "left" things for the other to "clear up." This is the master-slave relationship, but on the radical assumption that D and C were the same, Greg's passage can be read without change, and with the uncanny effect of reminding us how one person's writing actually is done—writers have masters and slaves in themselves:

18. Edward Maunde Thompson, *Shakespeare's Handwriting* (Oxford: Clarendon Press, 1916); "The Autograph Manuscripts of Anthony Munday," *Transactions of the Bibliographical Society*, 14 (1919); "The Handwriting of the Three Pages," in *Shakespeare's Hand in the Play of Sir Thomas More*, which mentions a similarity between C and D on p. 111.

[Hand D] writes "other" and leaves it to C to assign the speech to whom he pleases. In ll. 233 and following he begins by writing a sentence which in the absence of punctuation it is almost impossible not to misread, then alters and interlines till it becomes impossible to follow his intention, and leaves it to C to clear up the confusion. This C does by boldly excising some three lines and inserting one makeshift half-line of his own.[19]

The writer is often at odds with himself, faced with clearing up his own leavings whether or not he will eventually be called a genius, and although in the collaborative work of the theatre for which *Sir Thomas More* was composed and revised, it is possible that C and D were different, in the scholarly work of authorial identification it is advisable to consider them the same, at least until the ghost disappears. For the ghostly identification of Shakespeare has not been laid to rest here. Shakespeare may well have collaborated on the original *Sir Thomas More* for Strange's men in 1592–1593, and the secret charm that will lay that spectre to rest is the counteridentification: not Shakespeare as Hand D, but Hand D as Hand C. What can a literary scholar say about that? There are no letters between D and C, no ground for the ghostly name to take shape.

That one Hand is the same as another eliminates the very synecdoche by which authors are thought to be seen behind manuscripts ("he threw up his hands and cried 'Shakespeare!' "). For the Hand is really a trope of another kind—not a synecdoche for the writer but a metonymy for the writing, the actual handwriting on the paper; and the handwriting does not come out of a grave, it comes out of the stacks in the Manuscript Division of the British Library, where nothing apart from some of the Supervisors is to be feared. Let Hand D possibly be Hand C, Anon and Shakespeare at once, the genius and the functionary. That is just one way of stating the assumption behind this book, that all the writing in the manuscript of *Sir Thomas More*, even the censor's, holds to the similarity of addressing the co-

19. Greg, ed., Malone Society Reprint, p. xiii.

herent work of the Elizabethan theatre. I think the manuscript can be understood more clearly on that assumption, and can be described in its probable historical place. It was originally written for Alleyn and the large, risk-running company of Strange's men in 1592–1593. It was revised and cut down a decade later for the Admiral's men, when they were reviving Alleyn's big roles at the Fortune. The evidence for these assertions comes from the theatrical characteristics implied by the manuscript and does not depend upon knowing the authors' identities. What can be said about the authors' identities strengthens these assertions but is not necessary to them: let Munday, Chettle, and Shakespeare be the collaborators on the original version; let Dekker, Heywood, and perhaps Chettle be the revisers a decade later; let Hand C be present on both occasions, a writer essential to the others; and these names fit easily into the pattern of theatrical characteristics.

A final word should look to broader possibilities, however, and the broader possibility that emerges from our study of Hand C and Hand D is that, belonging to one intention, the presumed genius and the presumed functionary should be recognized in each other. If the master and the slave can be seen as one, the distance between C and D becomes an interior space, a space known to you and me as well as the others, and our need for ghostly authors should disappear once and for all.

Appendix

Minimum Casting Charts for Plays Listed in Chapter 4

Included are speaking roles only. All changes under thirty lines are noted.

1 Honest Whore

1. Hippolito
2. Fluello
3. Duke   Roger   Hippolito's Servant
4. Castruccio   Fustigo
5. Sinezi   Dr. Benedict
6. Pioratto   Porter
7. Matheo   Crambo
8. Candido   3 Madman
9. 1 Servant   George   Sweeper   2 Madman
10. 2 Servant   Poh   Doctor's Man   Friar Anselmo
11. Officer   1 Madman

12. Bellafront
13. Infelice   2 Prentice
14. Viola
15. 1 Prentice   Mistress Fingerlock

2 *Honest Whore*
1. Hippolito
2. Orlando Friscobaldo
3. Candido
4. Duke 2 Vintner
5. Matheo
6. Beraldo
7. Carolo
8. Fontinell 1 Servant
9. Astolfo
10. Lodovico
11. Bryan 1 Vintner Master of Bridewell
12. Antonio Giorgio 1 Guest Constable
13. 2 Servant Bots
14. Bellafront
15. Infelice
16. Bride Catherina Bountinall
17. 1 Prentice Penelope Whorehound
18. Mistress Horseleech Dorothea Target[1]

Whore of Babylon
1. 1 Cardinal Plain Dealing
2. 2 Cardinal 4 Footman Albanois
3. 3 Cardinal Herald
4. 4 Cardinal Cousin
5. Prologue 1 King
6. 2 King
7. 3 King Campeius
8. Truth
9. Time Paridel
10. Fidili Palmio
11. Florimell Conjurer Ragozzini
12. Elfiron Campeggio Captain (V, v)
13. Parthenophil Gentleman
14. Ropus
15. Empress[2]

---

[1]Boys' roles could be reduced to four, but this would require further doubling within the procession of prostitutes in V, iii. The doubling of Mistress Horseleech and one of the prostitutes, shown above, would be avoided with a sixth boy.

[2]The last three assignments are certainly for boys. The sexual division of some earlier roles cannot be decided.

16. Titania
17. Aura

The Roaring Girl
1. Sebastian
2. Alexander
3. Goshawke   Porter
4. Greenwit   Tearcat
5. Trapdoor
6. Openwork   Sgt. Curtilax   2 Cutpurse
7. Gallipot   1 Cutpurse
8. Tiltyard   Yeoman Hanger   Sir Thomas Long
9. Beautious Ganymede   Adam Appleton   Gull
10. Lord Noland   Laxton   Tailor
11. Sir Fitz Allard   Neatfoot   Coachman   3 Cutpurse
12. Prologue   Epilogue   Davy Dapper[3]   Jack Dapper
13. Fellow (II, i)   Servant (V, ii)

14. Moll
15. Mary Fitz Allard
16. Mistress Tiltyard
17. Mistress Openwork
18. Mistress Gallipot

Thomas Lord Cromwell
1. Cromwell
2. Hodge   More   2 Merchant   2 Witness   Sgt. at Arms   Sadler
3. 1 Smith   Host   Hales[4]   Seely   Mess. (V, i)   1 Citizen   Officer (V, v)
4. 2 Smith   Governour (II, iii)   Mess. (III, ii)   Suffolk
5. Old Cromwell   Chorus   Lieut.
6. Bowser   Governour (III, ii)   Wolsey   1 Merchant   1 Witness   Herald
7. Bagot   Gardiner
8. Fryskiball   Mess. (III, iii)   2 Citizen   Hangman
9. Banister   Bedford
10. Post (II, i)   Mess. (III, ii)   Norfolk   Usher   Servant (IV, v)

11. Banister's Wife   Young Cromwell
12. Seeley's Wife

[3]Briefest change: 26 lines.
[4]Briefest change: 18 lines.

163

Hamlet, Quarto of 1604–1605.

1. Hamlet
2. Claudius   Ghost
3. Horatio
4. Bernardo   Reynaldo   Guildenstern[5] 2 Player (III, ii)
   Capt. (IV, iv)   Mess. (IV, v–vii)   Engl. Amb.
5. Francisco   1 Ambassador   1 Player   2 Gravedigger
   Osric
6. Marcellus   Gentleman (IV, v–vi)   Priest   Fortinbras
7. 2 Ambassador   Sailor (IV, vi)   Lord
8. Laertes   Rosencrantz
9. Polonius   1 Gravedigger
10. Gertrude
11. Ophelia
12. Boy Player

[5]Briefest change: 22 lines.

Index

Acting companies:
court performances, 59–61, 70–
71, 121
leading actors, 61–66
political characteristics, 59–60
size, 56–58, 64–66
*See also entries for individual
companies*
Adams, John Cranford, 98n
Adams, Joseph Quincy, 124
Admiral's/Prince Henry's men, 57,
61–73, 78, 81–95, 116–124, 159
casting and doubling, 85–86, 90–
92, 94, 95n, 113–114
staging, 105–108, 112
Alchemist, The, 62
Alleyn, Edward, 16, 39, 61–64, 82–
84, 90, 92–93, 116n, 120, 146,
150, 159
Alphonsus of Aragon, 116, 125, 130
Anon, 152–158
Anti-alien disturbances (1592), 67–
73, 94–95, 150
Antony and Cleopatra, 62

Armin, Robert, 92
Armstrong, William A., 98n
Atheist's Tragedy, 62

Bald, R. C., 25, 28, 50n, 51n, 65n,
143n, 144n
Baldwin, T. W., 18, 61
Barroll, J. Leeds, 98n
Battle of Alcazar, 116, 125, 126, 130,
132n
Beckerman, Bernard, 97n, 99n, 100n
Bentley, G. E., 35n, 79n
Bentley, John, 64
Berry, Herbert, 98n
Bevington, David, 46n, 78n, 106n
Blayney, Peter, 21, 24, 25, 26, 31, 32,
41, 50n, 65n, 137–138, 144n,
145, 147, 147n, 149
Blind Beggar of Alexandria, 82, 116,
125
Blind Beggar of Bednall Green, 115n,
117, 125
Blistein, Elmer, 117
Bond, R. Warwick, 120

Bowers, Fredson, 39, 119, 121, 122, 123
Bradley, David, 78n
Brandimer, 67
British Library (or British Museum), 15–17, 151
  Manuscript Students' Room, 16–17, 31–33, 158
  Supervisors of Manuscript Students' Room, 16–17, 19, 158
Bronze Age, 115n
Bryan, George, 61
Buc, George. *See* Master of the Revels
Burbage, Richard, 36, 61–64, 92

Candido, Joseph, 27n, 106n
Captain Thomas Stukley, 115n
Cartwright, William, 81
Cerasano, S. P., 116
Chamberlain's/King's men, 57–58, 62–73, 87, 95n
  casting and doubling, 87–88
Chambers, E. K. (footnote references not indexed), 37, 65, 70, 116–124, 147
Chambers, R. W., 16
Chapman, George, 119
Chettle, Henry, 16, 82–83, 87, 91, 93, 95, 117, 120, 121, 124, 135, 145–150, 159
  See also Hand A
Children of the Revels, 62
Chillington, Carol A., 23n, 95n
Clarke, P. W., 118
Clyomon and Clamydes, 60n
Comedy of Humours, 119
Condell, Henry, 155
1 Contention of York and Lancaster, 56n, 57
  See also 2 *Henry VI*
Coriolanus, 62

Daborne, Robert, 38–39
David and Bethsabe, 117, 126, 130
Davison, P. H., 40
Death of Huntington, 117, 127, 130
Dekker, Thomas, 16, 83, 91, 99n, 121, 122, 124, 135, 145–146, 159
  See also Hand E

Dessen, Alan C., 106n
Doctor Faustus, 82, 117, 125, 130
Doran, Madeleine, 106n
Downfall of Huntington, 57, 117, 130
Drayton, Michael, 122

Eccles, Mark, 95n
Edward I, 118, 127, 130
Edward II, 44
Elizabeth I, 68–71
Elizabethan theatre:
  actors' "parts," 34–42, 49–52
  casting and doubling, 43–52, 77–78, 86
  censorship, 17, 20, 38, 50–52, 66, 72, 94–95, 138, 143–144
  costumes, 53–54
  improvisation, 80–81
  largest plays, 41, 56–59
  longest roles, 61–66
  "plots," 34–40, 50, 56n
  political implications, 67–73
  promptbooks, 17–20, 34–40, 49–50
  rehearsal and textual practices, 16–19, 32–33, 34–41, 49–52, 53
  staging, 96–99
Englishmen for My Money, 124
Essex rebellion (1601), 69
Evans, G. Blakemore, 22, 23n

Famous Victories of Henry V, 57, 60n, 115n
Foakes, R. A., 66n, 83, 89
Folger Library, 148
Folio of 1623 (Shakespeare), 155
Forker, Charles R., 27n, 106n
Fortune playhouse, 81–82, 91–92, 112, 116, 117, 118, 121, 159
Fortune's Tennis, 83, 118, 125
Four Plays in One, 67, 122
Four Prentices of London, 115
Frederick and Basilea, 118, 125
Friar Bacon and Friar Bungay, 56n, 57, 60n, 67, 82, 118, 119, 125, 132n, 133n, 148

Gabrieli, Vittorio, 21n, 45n
Gair, Reavley, 98n

Galloway, David, 98n
*George a Green, The Pinner of
Wakefield*, 118, 125
Globe playhouse, 92, 97
Golden Age, 115n
Goodale, Thomas, 29, 42, 48, 65–66,
93–94
Green, M. A. E., 71n
Greene, Robert, 36, 119, 133n, 147–
149, 151
Greg, W. W. (footnote references not
indexed), 15, 17, 18, 25, 28, 32,
37, 38, 50, 51, 65, 67, 70, 80, 81,
116–124, 143, 152–157
Gurr, Andrew, 98n

Hamlet, 62, 81, 87–88, 164
Hand A., 16, 33, 76, 83, 93, 105,
135, 145
See also Chettle, Henry
Hand B., 16, 21–24, 28, 29, 30, 33,
42–52, 76–80, 83, 91, 93, 105,
111, 135–146
See also Heywood, Thomas
Hand C., 16, 21–33, 43–52, 65, 75–
80, 83, 87, 91, 93, 105, 110,
135–146, 154–159
Hand D, 16, 18, 21–24, 33, 42, 44,
48–49, 75, 83, 86, 93, 95n, 105,
135–159
See also Shakespeare, William
Hand E, 16, 27, 30, 32, 33, 43–52,
76–77, 83, 110, 135, 145
See also Dekker, Thomas
Hand S, 16, 28, 30, 33, 55, 83, 135,
142–143
See also Munday, Anthony
Harbage, Alfred, 55n, 57
Harry of Cornwall, 67
Hathway, Richard, 122
Haughton, William, 121, 124
Hays, Michael, 75n, 154
Heminges, John, 61, 155
Henry V, 62
2 Henry IV, 40
1 Henry VI, 57, 60, 67, 119, 126, 127,
133
2 Henry VI, 44, 56n, 57, 65n, 141
*See also 1 Contention of York and
Lancaster*

3 Henry VI, 44
Henslowe, Philip, 37, 38, 80, 90, 95n,
146
Diary, 56n, 66, 70, 76, 82–84, 93,
115–124, 148, 152
Herbert, Henry. *See* Master of the
Revels
Heywood, Thomas, 16, 49, 80, 83,
87, 91, 124, 135, 146, 159
See also Hand B
Hinman, Charlton, 119
Hodges, C. Walter, 98n, 99n
Hoffman, 95
1 Honest Whore, 85, 92, 107–108,
112, 161
2 Honest Whore, 85, 92, 162
Hook, Frank S., 118
Hosley, Richard, 98n, 99n
Howard-Hill, T. H., 37n, 39n, 65n,
87n, 95n, 140n
Humphries, A. R., 41n
Humorous Day's Mirth, 119, 125
Hunter, Dard, 75n

1 If You Know Not Me, 57
Ill May-Day uprising, 17, 18, 20, 22,
68–69, 72, 138
Ingram, William, 75n

Jackson, MacD. P., 87n
Jenkins, Harold, 18, 22, 23n, 28,
149n
Jew of Malta, 60, 62, 69, 82, 119, 127,
131, 133
John a Kent and John a Cumber, 65,
115n
John of Bordeaux, 56n, 67, 115n, 118,
119, 125, 133, 148
Jonson, Ben, 63, 93
Juby, Dick, 81
Jugurth, King of Numidia, 95
Jupiter and Io, 115n

Kempe, Will, 61, 92, 120
Kernodle, George, 98n
Kind-Heart's Dream, 147–150
King Leire, 60n, 119, 125
King, T. J., 98n
King's men. *See* Chamberlain's/King's
men

Knack to Know a Knave, 60, 67, 120, 125, 133, 153
Knack to Know an Honest Man, 120, 125
Knell, William, 64
Knutson, Roslyn, 66n, 116
Kyd, Thomas, 68, 73, 147–148, 152–153

Lady Jane, 122
Lake, D. J., 87n
Lawrence, W. J., 18n
Leicester's men, 59
Levin, Richard, 106n
Lodge, Thomas, 147–148
London Florentine, 83
Long, William, 65n
Longshanks, 82, 118
Look about You, 120, 125
Looking Glass for London and England, 60, 67, 120, 128, 131, 133
Lowin, John, 63–64

McKerrow, R. B., 121
McMillin, Scott, 56n, 57n, 58n, 119, 148n
Mahomet, 82, 116
Malcontent, 62
Marbeck, Thomas, 81
Marlowe, Christopher, 68, 73, 147–153
Massacre at Paris, 57, 60, 69, 82, 91, 120, 128, 131, 133, 150
"*Massacre at Paris* leaf," 148
Master of the Revels, 71
 George Buc, 94–95
 Henry Herbert, 38–39
 Edmund Tilney, 17, 20, 30, 50–52, 66, 72–73, 94–95, 138–140, 142–144, 150
Meagher, John C., 117n
Measure for Measure, 62
Melchiori, Giorgio, 21n, 22, 23n, 45n, 51n, 65n, 75, 103n, 140–142, 143n
Metz, G. Harold, 106n, 137n
Mulomurco, 152
Munday, Anthony, 16, 65, 82–83,

87, 91, 117, 120, 122, 135, 140–141, 144–150, 159
See also Hand S

Nagler, A. M., 98n, 99n
Nashe, Thomas, 60n
Newington Butts playhouse, 70
Nosworthy, J. M., 27n
Nungezer, Edwin, 63n

Old Fortunatus, 121, 125, 131
Old Wives' Tale, 60n
Oliphant, E. H. C., 144n
Orlando Furioso, 121, 125, 133
 actor's "part," 36–40, 121
Orrell, John, 98n
Othello, 62

Pallant, R., 56n
Parr, William, 81
Patient Grissell, 99n, 121, 125
Peele, George, 147–148
Pembroke's men, 57, 62
Petti, Anthony, 154–157
Phillips, Augustine, 61
Pollard, A. W., 22, 33n, 65, 147n, 151–152, 155n, 156n
Pope Joan, 152
Pope, Thomas, 61
Porter, Henry, 124
Prince Henry's men. *See* Admiral's/Prince Henry's men
Privy Council, 68–70
Proudfoot, G. R., 75n, 120
Prouty, C. T., 117, 118

Queen Anne's men. *See* Worcester's/Queen Anne's men
Queen's men, 56n, 57–61, 64–73, 92, 118, 119

Rabkin, Norman, 106n
Red Bull playhouse, 97
Renwick, W. L., 119
Revenger's Tragedy, 62
Reynolds, George, 97, 98n, 99n
Rhodes, Ernest L., 98, 114, 115n, 117
Rhodes, R. Crompton, 37

Richard II, 69
Richard III, 62
Rickert, R. T., 66n, 83, 89
Roaring Girl, 85, 92, 163
Rose, Mark, 106n
Rose playhouse, 60, 65–73, 97, 99n, 112, 150–153
   staging, 113–134
Ross, Lawrence J., 99n
Rowley, Samuel, 82

St. Paul's playhouse, 97
Schoenbaum, Samuel, 55n, 57
Selimus, 60n
2 Seven Deadly Sins, 56n, 57–58, 64–67, 115n, 122, 125, 131, 133, 146
Shaaber, M. A., 40n
Shakespeare, William, 16, 36, 62, 67, 86–87, 93, 95n, 136, 140, 148–159
   See also Hand D
Shapiro, I. A., 65n
Shoemakers' Holiday, 122, 125
Silver, Brenda R., 152n
Silver Age, 115n
Simpson, Percy, 122
Singer, John, 80–84, 89, 92–93
Sir John Mandeville, 67, 152
Sir John Oldcastle, 57, 122, 125
Sir Thomas More (manuscript):
   Addition I, 20, 30, 40–41
   Addition II, 20, 21, 22, 23, 24, 43–52, 80, 136–145
   Addition III, 25–30, 43–52, 76, 79
   Addition IV, 25–30, 32, 43–52, 76, 110
   Addition V, 25–30, 42–52, 76
   Addition VI, 29–31, 42, 44–52, 76, 80
   errors, 19–31, 40
   lacunae, 20, 25
   location, 15–17, 31–33
   watermarks, 74–75
Sir Thomas More (play):
   casting and doubling, 42–52, 76–79, 111
   number of roles, 54–56

sources, 20–21
staging, 97–112
Sir Thomas Wyatt, 115n, 122–123, 125
Sisson, C. J., 23n, 28n, 95n
Smith, D. Nichol, 119, 123
Smith, Irwin, 98n
Spanish Comedy, 152
Spanish Tragedy, 44, 60, 62, 68, 82, 90–91, 123, 126, 128, 131, 133
Spevack, Marvin, 61
Spikes, Judith Doolin, 106n
Stanley, Ferdinando (Lord Strange), 71
Stevenson, Allan, 75
Strange's men, 56n, 57–73, 82, 91–93, 146–153, 159
   staging, 113–134
Streitberger, W. R., 95n
Sussex's men, 57, 118, 119, 123
Swan drawing, 99, 126, 129, 132

1 Tamar Cam, 80–82, 89–93, 115n, 123, 125
1 Tamburlaine, 44, 58, 123,
2 Tamburlaine, 44, 58, 62, 123, 128, 131
Taming of the Shrew, 57
Tannenbaum, S. A., 65n, 94n, 147n
Tarlton, Richard, 60n, 61
Taylor, Gary, 60n, 78n, 83n, 87n, 95n, 156n
Thomas Lord Cromwell, 82, 87–88, 163
Thompson, Edward Maunde, 65n, 151–157
Thorndike, Ashley, 98n
Three Lords and Three Ladies of London, 60n
Tilney, Edmund. *See* Master of the Revels
Timon of Athens, 62
Titus Andronicus, 44, 123, 126, 128, 131
Troilus and Cressida ("plot"), 124, 128, 131
Troublesome Reign of King John, 60n
True Tragedy of Richard III, 57, 60n
Two Angry Women of Abington, 124, 125

Van Fossen, R. W., 124
Velz, John, 65n
de Vocht, H., 120
Volpone, 62

Walker, Alice, 41n
Walsingham, Francis, 59
Warren, Michael, 156n
Webster, John, 122
Wells, Stanley, 78n
Wentersdorf, Karl P., 65n

When You See Me You Know Me, 62–
    63, 82, 84–85, 92, 106–107, 112
Whore of Babylon, 85, 92, 162
Wickham, Glynne, 98n
Wilson, J. Dover, 18, 37, 151–152
Wilson, Robert, 120, 122
Wiseman of Westchester, 65
Woman Killed with Kindness, 124, 125
Woman Will Have Her Will, 124, 129
Woolf, Virginia, 152–153
Worcester's/Queen Anne's men, 57,
    63–64, 83, 122–123, 124

Library of Congress Cataloging-in-Publication Data

McMillin, Scott.
    The Elizabethan theatre and The book of
Sir Thomas More.

    Includes index.
        1. Sir Thomas More (Drama) 2. Theater—
England—History—16th century. 3. Shakespeare,
William, 1564–1616—Authorship. 4. Munday,
Anthony, 1553–1633—Authorship. 5. More,
Thomas, Sir, Saint, 1478–1535, in fiction,
drama, poetry, etc. I. Title.
PR2868.M37 1987   822'.3   86-47996
ISBN 0-8014-2008-3–(alk. paper)